*Big Sugar* (1989)

*Moonshine* (1985)

*Midnights* (1982)

# The Riverkeeper

 ALFRED A. KNOPF   NEW YORK   1991

# The Riverkeeper

## ALEC WILKINSON

THIS IS A BORZOI BOOK
PUBLISHED BY ALFRED A. KNOPF, INC.

Copyright © 1986, 1987, 1990 by Alec Wilkinson
All rights reserved under International and Pan-American Copyright
Conventions. Published in the United States by Alfred A. Knopf, Inc.,
New York, and simultaneously in Canada by Random House of Canada
Limited, Toronto. Distributed by Random House, Inc., New York.

"The Blessing of the Fleet" (1986), "The Riverkeeper" (1987), and portions
of "The Uncommitted Crime" (1990) were originally published in
*The New Yorker*.

Library of Congress Cataloging-in-Publication Data
Wilkinson, Alec.
The riverkeeper / by Alec Wilkinson.—1st ed.
    p.   cm.
Contents: The blessing of the fleet—The riverkeeper—The uncommitted
crime.
    ISBN 0-394-57313-7
    1. United States—Social life and customs—1971- 2. Portuguese
Americans—Massachusetts—Cape Cod—Social life and customs.
3. Seafaring life—Massachusetts—Cape Cod. 4. Cape Cod (Mass.)—Social
life and customs. 5. River life—Hudson River (N.Y. and N.J.) 6. Hudson
River (N.Y. and N.J.)—Social life and customs. 7. Tlingit Indians.
8. Admiralty Island (Alaska)—Social life and customs.
    I. Title. II. Title: Riverkeeper.
E169.04.W54   1991            90-53423   CIP
973—dc20

Manufactured in the United States of America
First Edition

*For*

SARA BARRETT

*and*

HUGH COSMAN

# CONTENTS

*The Blessing of the Fleet*

THE MAJORITY OF FISHERMEN IN THE FISHING fleet of Provincetown, Massachusetts, are clannish, irascible, and devout. Aboard many of their boats is a crucifix or a religious medallion or a plaque with a picture and a pious inscription. "O Lord, My Boat Is So Small, and Your Sea Is So Big" is a popular inscription. The better part of the fishermen are Portuguese or of Portuguese descent. They imagine conspiracies. They are frequently solemn and deeply cynical; they are fond of saying, "Life is a bitch, and then you die." They believe that a hatch cover placed upside down is a portent of trouble, that a knife stuck in a mast invites evil, and that whistling aboard a boat calls the wind.

Some are the descendants of men from the Azores and the Cape Verde Islands; during the middle of the nineteenth century it was the practice of Provincetown whalers to stop at those islands and augment their crews. Some are the offspring of men who in the late nineteenth century and the early part of this one spent months at a time aboard Portuguese schooners fishing the Grand Banks. The schooners launched fleets of dories, which spread out over the banks in a line. The sailors who manned them were known as Grand Bankers. Now and then, a Grand Banker would intentionally row off in a fog and ship his oars and wait to be rescued by a Provincetown or a Gloucester or a New Bedford boat. Some of the fishermen were born in Portugal but arrived in this country as children and have never been back; a visit to the town of their birth is often the ambition of their retirement. Some are a generation or two removed from Portugal but consider themselves Portuguese, and look unmistakably so, because their bloodlines are pure. Some have been in Provincetown only a few years, and speak almost no English, and have no intention of learning any. They spend most of their time on the water, and when they stop on land they tend to remain within the Portuguese community. When they have a piece of business to transact—a tax form to answer or a credit application to complete—they find someone who can translate.

Provincetown is at the end of Cape Cod. Approximately thirty-five hundred people live there year round. At times, the Portuguese have accounted for as much as three-quarters of the town's population. At the moment, they are probably half. It is a narrow town. The houses are simple and austere and are built close together. It is settled mainly around its harbor, which is unusually deep and sound. Two streets—Commercial Street, which is the main street, and Bradford Street—run the length of the town. Until the early nineteenth century, there were only streets that ran back from the harbor. A person travelling from one end of the town to the other had to do so by way of the beach. Houses by the water had their front doors facing the harbor. When the path was laid for Commercial Street, some of the citizens rotated their houses on their foundations so that the front doors faced the street. From the water, the skyline of the town is mainly low and horizontal, broken only by the steeples of the town hall and several churches, and by the tower of the Pilgrim Monument. The light that falls on the harbor and the town has a particular lustre, which has long been attractive to painters. Provincetown is almost an island, and what accounts for the quality of the light is the great plains of water that edge it and reflect the sky.

The original names of many of the first Portuguese have disappeared. Some took those of captains they sailed under or worked for ashore, some changed their names to more English-sounding ones, and some became known under nicknames that fell into general use. Costa, Duarte, Joseph, Macara, Souza, Medeiros, Tasha, and Taves are common names in the town. The practice of leaving the harbor for a day or two at a time and fishing on the ocean and then shipping the catch fresh to the market was begun by the Portuguese. It started as an occupation of the late fall and winter, the off-season on the Grand Banks. The Portuguese fishermen have the reputation among the rest of the fleet of being tireless workers and fearless of weather. Some of them will stay on the water for days at a time, following schools of fish through storms, and sometimes returning to land only long enough to unload their catch and refuel. The Americans in the fleet tend to buy their homes. The Portuguese generally rent. They often buy real estate in Portugal—one man in the fleet owns an apartment building near Lisbon. If they have teen-age daughters, they frequently send them to relatives in Portugal, with as much faith and certainty in the outcome as if they were sending them to a convent.

The Portuguese of the purest blood have black hair and dark eyes and dark skin. To the summer community they are aloof and all but invisible. They stay home. They live back from the main part of town, in a neighborhood of newer houses, at the center of which is the Catholic church, and, except for the amusement of watching the summer crowds, they generally avoid the congestion of traffic downtown. They trim their hedges and water their lawns and watch television. They are not especially given to curiosity. The mother of one fisherman lived twenty-one years on the west end of town and recently moved a mile or so away, to the east end. On her first day out shopping, she became lost, and had to call for someone to take her home. The fishermen keep different hours from those of the rest of the town. One occasionally sees their solitary figures among the summer crowds. They walk with purpose, and do not look like people who are on vacation—or like people who would pick Provincetown if they were. Their moment of public celebration is the Blessing of the Fleet, which takes place each year over the last weekend of June. No local girl is crowned Queen of the Fleet, and no essays are written in the schools about the importance of fishing, but there are several private affairs for the fishermen and their families, there is a parade, there is a prize for the best-decorated boat (won last year by the Liberty), there is a carnival mood, and there is a sense of tradition and continuity and alliance and renewal.

THE Provincetown fleet consists of thirty-five boats. All of them are draggers, of which there are approximately equal numbers of two kinds—Eastern-rigged and Western-rigged. Both are of the same proportions: they are high-bowed and broad-shouldered, like dories; they are generally between forty-five and sixty feet long; they have gently sloping decks; and they are built close to the water. Western-rigged boats have their pilothouses forward; Eastern have them aft. Western-rigged boats generally launch their nets from the stern, and Eastern-rigged boats launch them over the side. In retrieving them, Western-rigged boats move forward in the water and into the wind to keep the net free of the propeller. Eastern-rigged boats must come to a stop and turn broadside to the wind to prevent the net from drifting underneath them. They are thus always at a disadvantage in a heavy sea—particularly when the net is full and swaying above the deck. Western-rigged boats are preferred and are newer. As time goes on the Eastern-rigged boats are disappearing. Last year's program for the blessing had on its cover a photograph of the Liberty. The Liberty is owned by Nobert Macara. His sons Jack and Rick run it for him. Jack was the co-chairman of the blessing. The Liberty has its pilothouse forward, and so is a Western-rigged boat, but is unusual in that it launches its nets from the side. It was built in 1941, in St. Augustine, Florida, and it is also called a Southern-style boat, because it is a kind that is commonly used for shrimping in the South.

Half the fleet is built of wood, and half—the newer half—is of steel. The Liberty has a frame of oak and a hull of cypress. It was built without caulking. When the hull of a cypress boat is completed, it is sunk for several days. The cypress swells, and the hull then is raised, and emptied out, and floated. A wooden boat can change hands for as little as forty-five thousand dollars, but at that price it will probably need work. The boats remain in the fleet or are sold to members of neighboring ones or, like the Liberty, are passed down among families. Steel boats are often bought new. Most are built in Southern shipyards, and cost as much as four hundred and fifty thousand dollars. Some are immense. There are four big boats in the Provincetown fleet—the B. Trio, the Paula and Mark, the Ruthy L., and the Divino Criador. They fish in deep water, and stay out on the grounds several days at a time.

How early a captain leaves the harbor, how far he travels to reach his grounds, the determination he applies to his hours on the water, how often he fishes, and the chances he takes on the weather depend only partly on his ambition and the qualities of his boat. The fishermen have a saying to explain what decides the intensity of their schedules: "It's not the length of the boat, it's the size of the note." Many of the older boats are paid for. Wooden boats are built to last twenty-five or thirty years, but many in the fleet are older than that. Some are as much as fifty years old, and one is a hundred. The older boats are creaky. They look fragile. They look as if they could be shaken to pieces. They take a terrific pounding over the years. There is a lot of vibration. They loosen up. The nets they drag are held to the sea bottom by otter boards—tabletop-size slabs of oak bound in steel, or of plain steel. The otter boards are also called doors, and when the net is out of the water they are hung from steel frames on deck called galluses. On the Liberty, when the doors go over the side you can see the floorboards underneath the galluses heave. Every few years, the older boats spend a part of each spring on the rails at the boatyard. The captains do what they can to keep them in service, because the prospect of taking on the payments for a new boat is daunting.

An additional cost of operating a boat is insurance.

Premiums can be as high as forty thousand dollars a year. A boat on which money is owed is a boat that must carry insurance. Some of the older captains who have paid off their loans carry no insurance at all. This is the case with the Liberty. The members of the fleet buy coverage through an agency that insures boats all along the coast. They are part of a risk pool that includes other New England ports. Shortly before the blessing, because of a number of suspicious sinkings in other ports the insurance was canceled. Some of the captains were able to continue fishing by obtaining second mortgages on their homes and paying off the loans on their boats. Many captains with mortgaged boats were forced to fish anyway, though it was prohibited to do so without insurance. If they hadn't, they would surely have lost their boats. Because of the problem with insurance, some of the boats sat out the last blessing.

Some boats have absentee owners—at least one belongs to the widow of a fisherman—and some are owned by retired fishermen, who let them out for a share of the profits, but the majority are owned by their captains. A few of the captains are elderly—one is eighty-three—and have fished as many as fifty years around Provincetown. The elderly captains look nimble and much less than their age. The size of the fleet is not stable. Boats come and go according to the prosperity of the season. Ten years ago, when enormous beds of scallops were discovered off Chatham, everyone turned to scalloping, and twenty boats were added in a year. The beds have since been depleted, and many of the boats have disappeared.

The boats are painted bright colors. They look festive. One of them, the Barracuda, has an acid-green hull on which, running halfway toward the stern from the bow, is painted a gaping watermelon-red mouth with sharp

white teeth. Some boats have Portuguese names: the An-
cora Praia, the Divino Criador, the Divino Mar, the Little
Natalia; some names are dynastic: the Raider III, Mary
Ann VII; some are inspirational: the Liberty, the Liberty
Belle; some are devotional: the Guardian Angel, the St.
Jude; some are obscure: the Silver Mink, the B. Trio; and
a number are sentimental: the Ruthy L., the Sarah Lynn,
the Suzy & Sandra, the Jimmy Boy, the Josephine G., the
Charlotte G., the Joan & Tom.

THE program for last year's blessing contained pictures
and text and advertisements. It had a dedication of some
length to the late Insley Caton and to his late father-in-
law, Antone Joseph. The dedication was written by Betty
V. Costa. It says, "These two men, of different birth-
places, generations, and experiences, are now part of the
history of fishing in Provincetown. Each has left an in-
delible mark. May they enjoy eternity with the Great
Fisherman and may their families find solace and pride in
the heritage they left behind." It also says that Insley Caton was born in Provincetown in 1925, and that "in his
early years the traits that were to make him a multi-faceted
man were already evident." In high school he was an altar
boy and a basketball player, he liked music, and, as a senior, he was voted best boy dancer in the class. He joined
the Navy, and, after his service, came back to Provincetown, where he worked for the Suburban Gas Company
and then ran a restaurant before "embarking upon what
was to be his career, fishing." He married Antone Joseph's
daughter, Leona, and they had three sons. Throughout his
life, he attended dance classes with Leona and friends. He
had a laugh that encouraged people to laugh with him.

## II

He was considerate. When he wasn't fishing, he often attended daily Mass. He loved driving and travel and new experiences. He worked on various boats and then bought his own, the Leona Louise, which he ran for fifteen years. When he sold it, he went to work on a boat owned by one of his sons. He had intended to paint when he retired, and had bought an easel and some paints, but died before he was able to begin.

Antone Joseph was born in Portugal in 1897. He came to America at twenty-one, having already fished out of Portugal and Gibraltar and worked aboard a whaler. In Provincetown, he shipped as a doryman on the Grand Banks and later had a place on a dragger. He was married to Louisa Perry for forty-five years, and they had two daughters and two sons.

The program says:

> Although blessed with a sense of humor, Tony Joseph was shy and shunned the spotlight when the family gathered, preferring the sidelines, but enjoying the love and banter.
>
> On a visit to Portugal his wife, Louisa, was killed in an automobile accident and his was the sad task of bringing her home for burial. . . . He went to stay with Leona and Insley, who was like another son to him. He shared their home for about two years.
>
> Although he had little formal education, he was an intelligent man, not given to rash decisions. He went back to Portugal for a visit. After thinking it over carefully, he decided that for economic reasons he would remain and make his home there. He sold his Provincetown home and began his new life in the land of his birth. Later, he remarried. When his beloved Insley died, he came back for the funeral. There had been a

great bond between these two men. Fishing, love of family, and a father-son relationship had fused this bond.

Joseph visited Provincetown during the summer of 1984, passing the time with his family and the fishermen on the wharf, and in visits to the cemetery.

One afternoon during the blessing, I went to see Alice Joseph, who is married to Antone's son Anthony. I took with me a copy of the program, which I had just bought for a dollar at the L & A Market. Mrs. Joseph is a small, fragile woman with a round and pretty face. She has gray hair worn short and tightly curled. She is hobbled by arthritis, and she sits most of the day on her couch in the living room with the phone beside her. When someone arrives, it takes Mrs. Joseph a while to cross to the door and unlock it. She walks with a cane, and her progress is uncertain. Her head stays down, watching her path. A slight rise in the rug is an obstacle. Her house is on Bradford Street—the back street—near the town hall. The windows of the living room face the street but are high above it, so that a person sitting on the couch does not see it, only hears it. In many of the windows on the first and second floors, there are statues of fishermen.

Mrs. Joseph is recently retired from the position of town librarian. Over the years, she collected a lot of information about fishing—about studies, about the fleet, about wrecks, and about proposals in the statehouse. We talked in her living room. She showed me pictures from a past blessing. In one, she stands on the deck of her husband's boat among several people, and it is possible to see from it how pretty she was and how people were drawn to her vitality. She told me that the original grants of land in the town had been given from the harbor across to the ocean and that this partly accounted for the bunched-up, linear construction of the town: when a son married, his parents gave him land to build on behind their own; this provided the women with the comfort of each other's company while their husbands were away fishing. She told me that before electronic fish finders made it easier to locate fish captains would keep thorough records of sightings of schools and of the weather and the temperature of the water in order to try to predict their movements. She said fishermen rarely lived to see their children grow up, "but if they survive long enough, it seems to renew all the ties."

Her husband, Anthony, came in. It was his day off, and he had been out visiting. He had been a fisherman most of his life but had given it up two years ago and taken a job with the town as a parking-lot attendant. This was the result of a misfortune. He had bought a boat that turned out to need more repair than he had expected. The insurance company refused to accept it for coverage, and it was declared a total loss. He is still paying for it. "If we had all the money we've lost on fishing boats, we'd be well off," Mrs. Joseph said. Anthony is small and gaunt. His face is weathered, and his expression is fierce and remote and morose. He had on a windbreaker, a flannel shirt, and khaki pants. Mrs. Joseph said he would tell me about fishing. He didn't say anything. He sat in a chair at right angles to me and stared at me askance through thick glasses. Then he looked away. Then he looked back. He lit a cigarette and watched the smoke disappear into the air. I thought perhaps he had no intention of saying anything and was waiting for me to go. Then he said, "As soon as a man gets away from the sea, he is lost. Because God meant his disciples to be fishermen." He drew on his cigarette. "When he comes to the wharf, the fisherman doesn't *sell* his fish," he said. "He gives it away. I got thirty cents a pound for a fish that you go to the store and they sell it for six dollars."

In an attempt to cheer him, his wife showed him the program. "Look at what a good job they did, Anthony," she said. "Have you seen this? It's your father." She handed him the program, but he just waved his hand before him in the air and said, "Aaah, I don't want to live in the past."

H I S T O R Y : In the eighteenth century, a tax on the Provincetown fishery supported the schools. The fisherman with the year's lowest catch spent the following year as schoolmaster.

T H E R E are two kinds of captains in the Provincetown fleet. The first is opportunistic, and pursues whatever is abundant—mainly whiting. The second disdains whiting and goes exclusively after flounder—fluke, yellowtails, witches, dabs, blackbacks, and four-o'clocks. Whiting is present in the millions. It is caught in bulk by the fishing fleets of Gloucester and Boston and New Bedford, all of which are larger than Provincetown's and catch many more fish. The volume of their catch determines the price at the market. Whiting's value fluctuates wildly. It is a fish that must often be caught by the ton to provide much of a profitable return to the boat. Large catches of whiting sometimes return less than the cost of fuel for the trip. The Sunday of the week before the blessing, one Provincetown captain left the harbor early and steamed five hours to grounds where he knew there were whiting. He fished all day and steamed back with three thousand pounds of it, for which he received ten cents a pound. His trip bill was three hundred and twenty-five dollars. Three days later, mainly because the Gloucester boats did not catch much of it, whiting paid forty-three cents a pound. The market for whiting is mainly among the inner-city sections of Baltimore and Philadelphia, and its competition is chicken. When the price of whiting surpasses that of chicken, people desert whiting. The fish buyers say that Frank Perdue controls the price of whiting. Buyers do not like to handle whiting. In addition to the frequent disappointments of its price, it takes a long time to unload from the boats, because there is so much of it. Furthermore, every boat bringing in whiting at a close-to-worthless price is one less boat bringing in valuable fish.

Flounder is the chancier catch. In fish markets and restaurants, much of it appears inaccurately described as sole, which is more expensive. No sole is caught in the waters fished by Provincetown boats or any Connecticut or Long Island or Gulf of Maine boats. What is called gray sole is actually witch flounder; lemon sole is the name given to blackback flounder of more than four pounds. Six or seven boxes of flounder—there are a hundred and twenty-five pounds to a box—are generally worth a deckful of whiting. Flounder fishing is considered easy work. A fisherman has to find them, of course, which means that he must know something about the habits and movements of the fish, but once among them he need only lower his net and sweep the grounds. Whiting is all kinds of work, because the nets fill up so fast.

What is caught by the Provincetown fleet in the greatest abundance is dogfish. A while ago, a captain caught nine tons of them in three minutes. Dogfish are a pest. They are a kind of small shark. They are an aggressive fish, and drive away others. Also, they tear up the nets with their skin, which is as coarse as sandpaper. The Provincetown fishermen have no market for them. What market there is is in Europe, and is handled through contracts held by Gloucester boats. The Provincetown fishermen pitchfork them back into the water. The dogfish survive. The boats also catch, in lesser quantities, pollack, cod, hake, ocean pout, skates, and goosefish. The wings are all they use of the skates; and of the goosefish they sell only the tails. Sturgeon and red snapper turn up as strays. The year before last, a number of boats fished for squid. They caught them in such quantity that the buyers were unable to handle them. Last year, several boats made arrangements to deliver squid to Spanish and Italian processors waiting offshore, but the squid never showed up.

The boats leave the harbor between two and five in the morning, depending on the distance to the grounds their captains plan to fish, and they return by five in the evening, to have their catch unloaded onto trucks heading for the markets in New York, Boston, Philadelphia, or Baltimore—the destination depends on where the buyers found the best price. Where the boats fish depends partly on the season and partly on what their captains are after. Sometimes the fishermen work a certain area day after day, and sometimes they wake up having no idea where they will fish, and make up their minds on the trip from their houses to the harbor.

Provincetown boats, like all draggers, tow otter trawls—long, baggy cone-shaped nets that have been in use without alteration since the middle of the nineteenth century. A weighted line called a foot rope holds the base of the net to the bottom, and a line buoyed by floats, called the head rope, suspends the top of it. The head rope forms an arc, which at its widest point is between ten and fifteen feet. The rise of the arc is an advantage, because fish tend to strike upward when alarmed. A net is held open at its mouth by the doors, one on each side, rigged in such a fashion that the resistance of the water planes them out. Wooden doors weigh between seven hundred and fifty and eight hundred pounds; steel doors weigh twice that. The doors are a hazard. Coming out of the water, they have tremendous momentum, and can knock a person unconscious and overboard, or cut off fingers, or crush a hand. Many of the accidents that take place aboard fishing boats involve the doors.

By the time chains, lines, and doors are attached, a net costs between four and five thousand dollars. It can last for years, but it is easy to lose one, and even easier to tear one up. Nets snag on wrecks and rocks and anchors—practically any obstruction. There are scores of wrecks off the Cape. Some are charted, and some are too new or too small to be. Some have shifted their locations in storms. Others have been dragged out of position by the enormous scallop boats that come through the grounds pulling huge metal rakes. When a fisherman finds a new wreck, he takes a bearing on it, notes its position in a log, and reports it to the rest of the fleet. Sometimes when a net hangs up, three or four draggers will collect in a line, stern to bow, and tug on it, but if it won't come free it has to be cut. Fishermen never know when they will lose a net. They say that when they throw one over the side it belongs to God and when they get it back on board it is theirs. The Provincetown fishery is called either a ground fishery, because it catches mainly bottom-dwelling fish, or a flat-net fishery. Boats usually carry two kinds of nets—flat nets and spacer nets. A flat net tows flush against the bottom, and is for use over grounds of sand or mud. A spacer net has rollers of hard rubber at intervals along its mouth in order to raise it above rocks and keep it from tearing itself to shreds. The bottom of each net of either kind is reinforced with lengths of colored fiber-glass rope, which are tied into the mesh by the fishermen and hang down from it in strands called whiskers. The collection of whiskers is called the chafing gear, which used to be made of cowhide until it became too expensive. Boats fishing for whiting carry a net of a smaller mesh. The regular fishing net has a five-and-a-half-inch mesh. A whiting net has a mesh of two and a half inches. A captain must have a pretty good idea of the kind of terrain he is fishing over if he is to preserve his nets. Many captains buy standard nautical charts, on which they outline precisely, in pencil, what they have learned to be the shapes of various stretches of bottom. The shapes look like islands. The nets are dragged at about two and a half miles per hour, although a boat in pursuit of a swift-moving fish, like pollack, has to tow as fast as it can. The net catches everything in its path, but many fishermen believe that numbers of fish sense its approach and flee, and that as many escape as are caught.

RAYMOND DUARTE, a fisherman: "I was born in Portugal, in Viana do Castelo, in the northern part of the country, in 1946. We lived on one end of the Lima River, and on the other end was Spain. I was two when we left. I remember very little—the shape of a room, certain sounds. I have seen pictures of the house I grew up in. They look familiar, and I think I can just figure out something about them, but I can't. In Portuguese, my name would be Ramao. I'm fifth in line in the family. There's Adélia, Joaquin, Manuel, Maria, Raymond, Jimmy, Vinnie, and Candy. One's a banker, one's a nurse, one's a carpenter, one's in health foods in New York City, one's a vice-president of an insurance company, one's a pharmacist, and one has a retail store in Connecticut. Out of eight, I was the only one who decided to go into the fishing business.

"My father came to Provincetown in 1948. Arthur Duarte, my great-uncle on my father's side, was fishing here, and he sent for my father. My father fished with him a season, then brought the whole family. I learned English in school. They put me in a classroom and I had to figure it out. I wasn't allowed to speak anything but Portuguese at home, and that made it awkward with my friends. In Portugal, my father had been a fisherman, using hand lines and gill nets mainly. Gill nets for herring and hand lines for octopus in the rocks off the shore. My mother would help tar the nets and stretch them out in the sun to dry.

"There were no engines on the boats—only sails. My father would go out before dawn with a piece of bread and an orange and stay out all day, and if there was no wind he'd have to row home. In Provincetown, my father worked with my great-uncle on the Josephina. After a while, he was made captain of the Sea Fox, and then the Charlotte G., which the owner had built for him in 1952. Later, he bought it, and he still has it. It's registered at fifty-six feet, and it was built in Blue Hill, Maine, out of oak. My father is sixty-three, and has fished for fifty-two years. My great-uncle is eighty-three, and he just bought a new boat, the Guardian Angel, a steel Western-rig, forty-two feet. He was retired five or six years, and it drove him foolish not to fish. He's having a hard time these last few weeks. I heard from him on the radio this morning. He said he's been out four days and he can't find enough to eat. And he's been all over the ocean.

"I started fishing summers on the Plymouth Belle, where I stayed until a place opened up full time on the Charlotte G. Later, I ran the Reneva and the Cathy Joe, and I also owned one, the Jenny M. I didn't name her. I bought her from somebody in Hyannis, and that was the name she had on her. When I first had her, I fished the grounds I learned from my father. Often the two of us would be out there sweeping them together. I also found places my father didn't like fishing. Not for any reason— he just didn't like to go there. How you find new grounds is you throw out the nets and see what comes up; you ask questions.

"In 1973, I was being passed a basket of fish down the fish hold—you carry them on your shoulders—and the boat rolled and I went up in the air and came down backwards like a horseshoe on a pin board, which is what contains the fish in the hold; we pile up the pin boards in slats, like a fence, and each time the level of the fish rises you put in another. My back hurt, but I kept on fishing. I thought I had only bruised it. But it got so I was always the last man on deck, because the pain was so bad. I fished that way for months, and then I finally discovered from the doctor that it was a ruptured disk. That's when they told me I couldn't go fishing as a crew member anymore, and that's when I bought a boat. I was captain then, and I didn't do any of the heavy lifting. I went two or three years like that before, with all the constant yanking and pulling, my back started bothering me again. Then I was in real trouble. When you have no education, and they tell you no more fishing, you feel like your legs have been cut from under you. I did what I could. I opened a fish store and ran it a couple of years, but I lost interest and told my wife I wanted to sell it. She said, 'What do you want to sell this money-maker for?' I just missed fishing. I would drive down to the wharf and hear the racket, and see the gulls, and the boats landing fish, and the water all stirred up, and I would want to go fishing.

"I quit school to go fishing. I learned to splice wire, I learned to cook for five men, I learned about the engine room and how to change oil. I learned about the nets. After a while, I knew enough that if a man was sick I could take his place for the day. If the engineer was sick, I would go out as engineer. If it was the cook, I would be cook. Those were in the days when boats had five-man crews. Nowadays, the cook and the engineer have been eliminated. Used to be there were so many fish that the boats couldn't handle them. All the fish now are getting caught outside, way offshore, by big trip boats out of New Bedford that are gone ten and twelve days at a time. You could put a Provincetown boat on the deck of a New Bedford boat. My father was a hard, hard man for a teacher. Anybody but me could make a mistake. He's all the time tinkering with his nets. He likes to add twine to get the shape he wants, and they regularly need repair. It's incredible to see him, he works so fast. It's like a sewing machine to see his hands moving. I would be holding the twine while he was mending, and if I wasn't going fast enough he would whack me with the mending needle across my knuckles and say, 'Pay attention!' I would go home with my knuckles bleeding. I once fished with him thirty-eight days. Several times, day and night, just coming home to unload—eat, sleep, get up, and go right back out. After a few weeks, I said, 'Captain, I need a rest. When are we going to take a break?' 'When the prices drop, we'll take it easy.' Come near the end of the thirty-eight days, I say, 'Captain, the prices have dropped,' and he says, 'I know—now we need to catch twice as many.' Another time, the back of the pilothouse caught fire, so I went to him and said, 'Captain, you know the back of the pilothouse is on fire,' and he said, 'We're only going to make one more tow.' I've worked with him in a hundred-

and-ten-mile-an-hour breeze. The wind was off the land, and we went in close to the beach to anchor. We put out two anchors and they didn't hold, so he decided to let out the nets—if we couldn't anchor up, then we'd fish. The sand was blowing off the beach and it felt like nails. We had a helicopter from the Coast Guard come over the top of us and they opened up their door and held out a big sign and it said 'Hurricane,' clear as a bell you could read it, and my father said, 'What do they want?' and I said, 'They say it's a hurricane,' and he said, 'Well, I know that.'

"My father is very knowledgeable about fishing and about the water. He told me never to lose my respect for the water or I would be lost. He told me never to worry about the white water—only the green, because that's where the weight is. Fishing with him, I learned to watch the sky for signs of weather. If you see birds rotating way up—turning small, tight circles and not flapping their wings—you're going to get a blow. If you come down to the pier and you see sand floating on top of the water, or lights reflecting off the water in the dark before dawn, or you are on the water and the land looms up—it looks twice as high as it usually does, and things you don't normally see, now you will see them—all of these are signs of an approaching easterly wind. He is also forever looking for sun dogs—little rainbows way up in the sky in the early morning, streaks of two or three colors, and wherever you see them that's where the wind is going to come from the next day.

"In my time, I've seen squalls, waterspouts. I've seen the water flat as a table, a beautiful day, sun was out, come a squall, come with that squall hail—it took us four hours to get to the grounds and twelve to get home. One time, my father was fishing at Great Round Shoal, off Nantucket Sound, and he was waist deep in fish. It was flat calm. My father was in the pilothouse watching the barometer. He said, 'I don't like what I see. Bring in the nets.' The crew said, 'But we're waist deep in fish.' They had a deckful of cod. They were getting rich. 'I don't care. I'm captain here. Bring in the nets.' By the time he had hit Highland Light, about seventeen miles from port, the winds were sixty to sixty-five miles per hour and from the northeast with high seas, and when he hit the harbor they were a hundred and fifteen miles per hour. The trysail, which is used to steady the boat, was ripped to ribbons. He was fishing the shoal with the Redstart, out of New Bedford—a big steel-hulled boat, a beautiful boat—and she said, 'There's a lot of fish out here, we're going to wait it out.' I don't know what she did—if she ran into shoal water, or what—but to this day they are still looking for the Redstart.

"The problem with fishing is that your life is not your own. You get up at three or four in the morning. You're constantly away from home. My first son I didn't even see grow up. My wife figured it out—one week, I was home twenty-four hours. The rest of the time you're forever waiting by the phone—you never know when you are going to get a call. My father called one time at Thanksgiving. If he got the weather report in the evening and they gave him bad weather for the next two or three days and he thought he could get the night out of it, he would go out and fish the night. The only thing that stopped him was Good Fridays. We would fish until Thursday midnight, and then the net would come out of the water. He was a fanatic about that. Add to that, when you have the responsibility of a boat you are never comfortable at home. You can't rest. It's on your mind constantly. The harbormaster will call in the middle of the night and say you parted lines, or you're taking on water, and you have to race to the pier to correct it.

"When I first went fishing, I got seasick for two years. It got so bad sometimes that I wanted to jump overboard. 'This business is not cut out for you,' my father said, and I said, 'Yes, it is.' I hung on, and then one day he came down to the wharf and let the lines go and said, 'I'm not going fishing. You are.' He must have called about fifty times that day on the radio, checking up. One time, he called and said, 'Where are you?' and I said, 'Off Nauset,' and he said, 'How deep?' and I said, 'Twenty-seven fathoms,' and he said, 'You're in a bad, bad place.' I said, 'What do you mean?' He said, 'You got a wreck at twenty-five fathoms, you got one at twenty-six, you got one at twenty-seven, and one at twenty-nine.' So I rang the bells and raised everyone up on deck and hauled the nets and steamed the hell out of there. I fished the rest of the day outside of the wrecks and came in with about eleven thousand pounds of yellowtails and blackbacks, and he was tickled.

"Why I put up with the seasickness I don't really know. I just liked fishing, ever since I was in grade school. My mother always knew where to find me—down at the wharf, or at the trap sheds, where the trap fishermen kept their boats and their nets. I see three or four kids hanging around the pier now that are hooked. They can't stay away. They are going to be fishermen."

RAYMOND is compact and wiry. He has a small face, a large nose, a broad mouth, and eyes that are dark and sleepy and mournful. His hair is black, and his skin is dark; he looks as if he were made out of leather. He is agile. At the moment, he is on leave from the fleet. For

how long he doesn't know. He has lately become a partner in Oceanic Seafood, one of the buyers. (There are two
buyers in town.) He joined Oceanic because the owner
was in danger of going out of business and asked for his
help. Raymond felt that having only one buyer in town
would be a disaster for the fishermen, so he agreed. For
Oceanic, Raymond fields the fishermen's complaints.
When they bicker over prices and make accusations, he
attempts to explain the buyer's position. His manner is
patient and resigned. The fishermen are provocative and
excitable and flamboyant. They gesticulate wildly. They
harangue. They have difficulty understanding how the
fish they deliver to the wharf could be valuable one day
and close to worthless the next, but they are in general
agreement that it must be the result of treachery or incom-
petence or conspiracy on the part of the buyers. Consequently, Raymond is occasionally on the receiving end of
a lot of animosity. Some of his former associates mistrust
him and consider him a traitor. He sometimes says, "I
never realized how good I had it fishing." As a rule, the
discussions are conducted in Portuguese. They generally
take place on Friday—payday. Raymond stands by while
Michael, his partner, hands out envelopes on which he has
written the names of the boats. In the envelope is a statement of the captain's catch for the week and a check based
on the price his fish returned at the market. When the
captains arrive, Michael or Raymond greets them and asks
how they are doing. Many of them are cordial, some are
taciturn and misanthropic, some say, "I'll tell you when I
see the statement." It is when they see the statements that
the discussions begin. The fishermen insist that the fish
they unloaded were classified incorrectly by the fish culler.
They claim that they worked the same grounds as So-and-
So and that his fish were called jumbo and theirs were

called peewee. There is no way for this to be possible, they say. If Raymond is engaged, impatience will sometimes overtake the fishermen and they will talk to Michael, in English. If they are unable to speak English, they will just stand there and burn.

On any other day, if a fisherman has trouble starting his car he will call Raymond. If a boat is a man short, Raymond will leave his office and go down into the fish hold and help unload the fish. If a fisherman has a problem with his winch, Raymond will see what he can do there. He recently helped a fisherman who had just arrived from Portugal find a house and fill out a request for a mortgage.

Of the thirty-five boats in the fleet, Oceanic deals regularly with about half. Perhaps four or five of these are loyal, and will unload their fish with Oceanic no matter what the price, either because they especially like Michael or Raymond or because it is in their nature to be reliable or because they figure that over time they break even, and don't see the sense in playing off one buyer against the other. When they do, they occasionally lose. Raymond says, "A couple of months ago, an old friend of mine comes to me and says Raymond Cabral, the other buyer, is promising him seventy cents a pound on his yellowtail. I said, 'I can't guarantee that. Be my friend, but take it if you want, because I can only pay you what the market offers.' So he goes over there, cursing me out as a cheapskate, and the next day Michael hits a home run on yellowtail, and now the guy's a screaming maniac over here saying I tricked him." The man Raymond helped with his house and his mortgage went the next day to the competition, because the price per pound was higher by a penny.

Michael Perel, Raymond's partner, grew up in Brooklyn and Queens. He has never been on a commercial fishing boat. He is unacquainted with the full range of fish that his business purveys. "Some of the fish, I don't even know what they are," he says. "I look in the box, I can't tell them." Michael has been involved in the business for three years. Before that, he and his wife, Helaine, who works with him, lived in Atlantic Highlands off Sandy Hook Bay, in New Jersey, and Perel was an accountant with an office in Manhattan and clients in the Fulton Fish Market. He drove to work. He had the use of season tickets for the New York Rangers. He was also an obsessed jazz fan. For these reasons, he felt that he could probably never live anywhere except within the vicinity of New York City, even though he despised the pace and the dirt and the traffic and the ill manners of some of the people. His decision to leave was made suddenly. He was driving to the city and listening to WRVR, at that time the city's top jazz station. No one had told him that RVR was switching its format to country music. He went into the Lincoln Tunnel shortly before noon listening to a saxophone player, and when he came out a man was singing in a Southern accent, to the accompaniment of strings, about having his heart broken. Perel started banging on the radio. He had a small fit. He pulled his car over and called the station. The lines were busy. Four days later, pretending to be someone interested in buying advertising time, he finally got through, and heard about the switch. A client of his in the market told him then about a fish-buying business for sale in Provincetown in which the client was interested. Michael and Helaine went and visited, bought the business at auction for the client, and agreed to run it. He was forty years old and was unaware of the difficulties of an outsider's doing business in a small New England town. On his best days, he is elated by the pure air and the calm of the town and the ease and the success and the future of his business. On other days, he appears despondent. At these times, he will occasionally say, "What I bought was a hornet's nest, with all the hornets walking around biting."

Michael tried for a year and a half to run the business on his own. He had trouble getting along with the Portuguese fishermen. They upset Helaine with the uncharitable quality of their accusations. "They scream and yell," he says. "They raise their hands. I have an English bulldog I used to bring to the office, but now I have to leave him home—he started getting upset and biting them. I would talk two hours to them and I couldn't get it across. I don't speak Portuguese, but I knew the gist of what they were saying to me, and it was not an endorsement." Michael decided to buy the business for himself. He felt he needed help from someone in the fleet and, after making a survey of the prospects, selected Raymond as the most level-headed. "Raymond goes out there and talks to them and says, 'You're ignorant. What are you bothering me with this for?' But he tells them in Portuguese, so they appreciate it."

Oceanic has its premises in a building at the end of a long pier. It is the former site of the fishermen's coöperative, which went bankrupt. The building is on stilts and is two stories high. It sways in the wind. In winter, there is little protection from the cold. The fish are bought downstairs. There are garage doors on two of the three sides that face the water. At the end of the day, the boats dock at the doors and winch up their fish a box at a time. Fish cullers sort them according to size. The fish cullers are paid by the volume of fish they unload. Once they have got rid of their fish, the boats tie up three and four deep beside the pier. Seagulls settle in the rigging.

Michael and Raymond share an office upstairs. There

are two metal desks, of the kind found in police stations and small-town newspaper offices; three chairs; and a filing cabinet. The office has Masonite paneling, linoleum on the floor, and a picture window through which Michael and Raymond can see the tops of the masts and the radar equipment that looks like television antennas, then the breakwater beyond, and the end of the Cape in the distance. Schools of bluefish enter the harbor and froth up the water when they feed. Seals visit. There are lobsters living among the rocks of the breakwater. Wind off the water stirs the papers on the two desks. The room's only adornments are an enormous striped bass that Michael caught in the surf off Sandy Hook, a calendar, and three snapshots tacked to the wall above Raymond's desk. In the snapshots appear the deck of a fishing boat loaded with cod: Raymond's best catch. He stares at it and says, "I would love to go out and do something like that today." Michael keeps two clipboards. One says "Sales" and the other says "Problems."

Fish cullers come into the office wearing hip boots and leave puddles and fish scales on the floor. They sit and talk for a while or say nothing and watch what's going on in the room.

The phone rings and Raymond answers. He listens, then turns in his chair. "Do we buy tuna?" Michael shakes his head. Raymond says, "No, I think Mike Cannistraro's buying all the tuna free-lance. You may be able to reach him at the wharf. . . . O.K." He hangs up and says, "Tuna. We don't need no tuna."

Michael says, "We got enough headaches already."

The phone rings. Michael answers. "Canadian fish? Don't threaten me with imports! You shake it and it comes off the bones. You can't sell that in your classy market."

Michael makes a call. "Hey, I dialed a wrong number.

You guys need any more fish? Give me an order, so I don't waste a phone call."

A Japanese man appears in the doorway and asks to buy one flounder. Michael sends Raymond off to find it. The Japanese man goes with him. Michael turns to a fish culler standing in a corner of the room and says, "One hundred thousand pounds of flounder we do last week, and he wants to buy one." Raymond returns. He says, "One flounder he took. He paid three dollars." Michael turns to the fish culler. He says, "Don't you tell anybody that. This fleet will hang us. Tell them that in the interests of cementing friendship and trust between our two countries I gave a flounder to a foreign dignitary."

A man who owns a restaurant stops by to pick up some fish for his bouillabaisse. From the window, Raymond watches him toss the fish into the bed of a pickup truck, where there is a box of vegetables. He says, "See, he's already got the broccoli in the back of the truck. His bouillabaisse will be half made by the time he gets home."

The fish cullers stand up to go, and often slip on the fish scales while they are crossing to the door. The stairs leading to the office are steep and shallow and slick as grease.

What Raymond would like is to open a fishermen's museum. He would put in it all the curious objects that he has brought up over the years in his nets and that are now crowding his basement. He would put a radar screen up over the entrance, so that people could see all the boats at work on the banks. And he would hire an old fisherman to sit in the museum all day and answer people's questions.

Raymond is uncertain of his commitment to the fish-buying business. "Who knows from here how long I will stay?" he says. "I never know what I'm going to do. My wife says I scare her. She says, 'I never know what you are going to do next.' " He misses fishing. At slack times, he sits in the office and stares out the window. If you ask him what is on his mind, he will sometimes say that he is thinking about tows he would like to make. Occasionally, while he is supervising the unloading of an especially prosperous haul he will ask the captain where he was trawling, and on hearing the reply he will say, "Hey, those are my grounds." Michael and Raymond are essential to each other; neither could make the business a success on his own. Michael, at his desk, looks over and sees his future in the expression on Raymond's face and the glaze in his eyes. "Don't even *think* about it," he says. "Forget about it."

N O B O D Y fished during the blessing. No fish were shipped. In New York, the demand was for whiting. The price was sky-high.

T H E custom of blessing the fleet was imported from Gloucester. In 1946, Seraphine Codinha—who died recently—traveled to Gloucester with his father-in-law and his family on their boat, the Sea Fox, to view the blessing there. Gloucester is fifty miles across the water from Provincetown. The trip took five hours each way. They went over on Saturday and came back on Sunday. They talked it up afterward among the fishermen in the Provincetown fleet and decided to have a blessing of their own. A committee was formed. Mr. Codinha did not remember who, but someone wrote the bishop asking if he would come and bless them. In Provincetown, during the blessing, the boats make a wide circle of the harbor before passing in front of the bishop, who stands on the wharf. In Gloucester, the boats are blessed at the pier. I spoke to Mr. Codinha at home. He had retired from fishing and owned a stand on the wharf selling ice cream and frozen yogurt. He was short and portly. He had a long face, and jowls. His expression was intelligent and melancholy. He had watery eyes. He kept his hands in his pockets. On the wall in his living room was a painting of a fishing boat. Recalling the past held no particular interest for him. He was raised in Gloucester. As a young man, he went to San Diego and joined the California tuna-fishing fleet. He came to Provincetown after the Second World War. His father worked as a Grand Banker and planned his own emigration. According to custom, he rowed away from the line in a fog and waited to be rescued by an American boat. Six days later, one arrived. This was 1918.

THE BLESSING: On Thursday night, a dinner was held at the Holiday Inn for the members of the fleet and their families. There were lovely dark-haired children running around the room. There was a strong sense of patriarchy. Some of the men wore four-in-hands with leather jackets. Between the wings of one man's collarbone was a gold crucifix on a chain. A ticket to the dinner cost seventeen dollars, and a hundred and sixty were sold. Jack Macara, one of the chairmen, wearing a coat and tie, greeted guests at the door. His wife, Jill, in a party dress, pinned a silk flower to each woman. The dinner took place in a room that was narrow and long and dark. It had a low ceiling, and there was the sound of a cash register working at the bar. Windows at one end looked out on a parking lot and, beyond it, a road running along the harbor, then the bay in the distance, and the sky pressing down flat against it. There were rows of tables with white tablecloths. On each table were candles and a basket of silk flowers, and each setting had a place card. Outside it was raining. Someone said that the banner strung for the blessing above Commercial Street in the center of town had blown down in the wind and ripped. There was a discussion about its repair. There was a discussion about the weather. "By Sunday, it will be beautiful," one man said. "This will all be forgotten history."

The dinner began with a buffet of clams and oysters on the half shell. Shortly after the buffet had been emptied for the first time, two priests from the town's Catholic church arrived, beneath umbrellas. They stood beside the buffet. A woman with gray hair talked to them. A number of women turned toward them with looks of fond approval. One of the priests was small and stocky and had a round red face and wore glasses, and the other was taller. The smaller was jovial, and the taller was shy. While the smaller priest talked with the woman, the taller stood beside him, inclining his head toward the conversation. He had the diffidence of a scholar. He held a plate with both hands in front of his chest. It made a circle of white against his black suit, and he tapped his fingers on the bottom of it. A man arrived from the kitchen carrying above his head a platter of shellfish. He set the platter down, and the people fell on it. The priests held themselves aloof for a moment and then shouldered their way in among the others. When the platter was empty and the people had dispersed, the shorter priest said "Did you get any?" and the other said "I sure did. I kept my hand moving."

After dinner, there was dancing. At one moment, several couples held the floor. The most prominent was an older man and woman. They were hardly moving. The man had his lips pressed against the side of his wife's head and was singing quietly into her ear.


FRIDAY: It is a custom of the blessing for the fishermen to drape banners and pennants and streamers and kites from the rigging of their boats. Where they have rust, they cover it with paint. One captain keeps a pine tree lashed to the top of his mast, and replaces it each year for the blessing. His name is Louis Rivers, but he is known in the fleet as Christmas Tree Louis. It was intended that the fishermen would decorate their boats on Friday morning, but the weather was cool and windy and gray, so they put it off. It rained heavily in the afternoon, then the wind shifted straight around to the southwest. The clouds broke. The color of the water changed from gray to blue. The clarity was extraordinary. Jack, Jill, and Rick Macara, and Claire—Jack's sister, and the oldest Macara child— came down to the pier and went to work on the Liberty. They ran flags up and down the stays and strung kites between the top of the mast and the pilothouse. The kites were made of red, yellow, white, or blue canvas in the shape of fish several feet long. There were twenty of them. Claire had sewn them over the spring, after discussing the project many times on the phone with her mother, in Florida. The Macaras have a condominium there. Jack hoped that the example of the Liberty would encourage other captains to begin. "It gets the ball rolling," he said. It happened also to be the only time he had to spare. The next morning, he had to supervise children's games, and, in the afternoon, he had to run the quahog party and then see to the softball game.

. . .

SATURDAY: Early in the morning, the sky was gray, and the white buildings and the roofs and the steeples of the town stood out clearly against it. There was a yard sale on the lawn before the Universalist church, and a bake sale at the firehouse. The women at the firehouse sat in the frame of the open front doors, in front of the bumpers of the engines, and sold cupcakes with white icing and little American flags on them.

The quahog party thrown by the fleet committee for the fishermen and their guests took place at the V.F.W. hall. A ticket sold at the door for six dollars. For an additional fifty cents, a person could buy a chance on a raffle of four bottles of liquor. Many people bought several dollars' worth of chances. Claire sat behind a card table by the door and sold tickets. Jack said that the policy was to let the fishermen eat first and then admit the public. Claire had with her a list of retired fishermen, who were served free. Claire is short, and has dark hair and a round face and smiles easily. She had been away from Provincetown for a number of years and had returned early that spring, with her husband, to live there. Because she had been away for so long, she had to ask many of the older fishermen their names in order to check them against the list.

The Macaras were totally in charge of the luncheon. "Jack and Jill set up the tables," Claire told me, "and that's Aunt Mary sitting over there with my mother and father and my brother Peter. Aunt Mary's the oldest—eighty-one. She and Uncle Ernest are Naomi's mother and father. Aunt Naomi is the second cook in the kitchen. Aunt Marsha is the first, and Rick's in there, too. It's a pretty big family, and practically all of them were, or are, fishermen. When I was a kid, the family had the Liberty Belle, the Victory II, the Three of Us. Later there was the Pat Sea, the Ruthy L., and—let's see . . . Dean—this is my brother Dean—what was Uncle Anthony's boat called, when he had a boat?"

"The Annabelle R.?"

"No. Jack, when Uncle Anthony had a boat, what was it called?"

"Papa Joe?"

"No, that's the Correias'. Anyway, I don't know what Anthony's boat was called, but my Uncle Joe had a boat called the Cap'n Bill. I would say that there were seven boats in the family, and there were nine children—six sisters, only two of whom didn't marry fishermen, and three brothers—so practically everyone had a boat."

From the kitchen, men and women carried away paper plates of quahogs and ears of corn, from which steam rose, and beer, picked from trash cans filled with ice. The old captains sat with each other. There was a stage at one end of the room. Beside the stage was a trophy case. Along the walls were photographs in frames of groups of men holding plaques and posed before monuments. There were paintings of fishing boats, and there was a portrait of Eisenhower. Ceiling fans turned. The floor was taken up by tables. There were several families with small children. One woman with a baby sat opposite her husband. She put the child between them on the table, like a centerpiece, and spoke to it softly in Portuguese. The Linguica Band played Portuguese music. Its members are elderly. There are three of them. They perform sitting down. They play guitar, mandolin, and accordion. Their repertoire is mainly instrumental, but occasionally the guitar player hums through a microphone. The mandolin player is Claire's

Uncle Anthony. He wears big gold rings on his fingers and smokes a fat cigar. The players are uncommonly poised. They took the stage and sat for a long time staring out at the banquet, giving the impression that the view from their seats was arresting. After some time, and without conferring, they suddenly began. There were long pauses between songs, during which they stared out at the audience. In the course of their performance, they changed hats and women's wigs.

While they played, Jack circled the room selling tickets for the raffle. Jill then picked the winners. Jack made a small speech of thanks and asked someone to volunteer to be chairman for next year's blessing. (No one did.) "Myself, I won't be doing it again," he said. The women from the firehouse arrived and sold cupcakes to raise money for life memberships in the V.F.W. post. ("On behalf of the Lewis A. Young Post 3152 Life Membership," one of them said, "I'd like to thank you all for letting us come here and solicit our cupcakes.") By this time, the families with children were beginning to pack up and leave. The woman retrieved her baby from the table. The food and the beer had made the rest of the crowd drowsy, and they sat staring absently into the air before them.

That afternoon, there was a softball game between the fishermen and the members of the Fire Department. The rules of the previous year's game had been that a person on base had to drink a beer before advancing or else he was out. A player who argued the umpire's decision had to drink a shot of tequila.

Late Saturday night, the sky above the water was broad and clear and immense. The harbor was still. A school of pogies circled beside the pier, stirring the water, turning one way and then another in unison, like a flock of birds. There was light on the harbor from a nearly full moon. The boats at anchor, with the moonlight behind them, were black against the water. From the deck of one, somebody launched fireworks. The trails of the rockets were red and green, and the colors reflected on the water like neon. Beneath a light on the pier, a man jigged for squid. The squid shot into the light pursuing minnows, and the man dangled a lure before them. On the pavement, the squid let out long exhalations of air, like sighs. They did this for some time past the point at which it seemed possible that they could still be alive. All the boats had been strung with pennants, and their decks cleared, and their nets folded and hung like drapes, and their tools put away. Some of them had bunting in folds across their pilothouses. Several had banners. One said:

> DEUS ABENCOE
>
> TODOS OS PESCADORES
>
> SUAS FROTAS

Back in town, the bars had just closed. Always, in Provincetown, during the hour or so after the closing of the bars the men who have failed to make connections come out and stand on the street or lurk in the doorways of stores or in the shadows of houses or pose for one another like statues. Or wander up and down the street with no apparent destination, like people in a procession. Some of them linger most of the night. On their way to work, before dawn, the fishermen pass them.

SUNDAY: The morning was clear and warm. Fog the color of cigarette smoke hung in a bank like hills off the backshore. At the pier, two men worked, putting up the metal framework of the bishop's stand. Several captains loaded ice aboard their boats for the parties that would follow the blessing. (The captains do not allow anyone on board to open a beer or a bottle of liquor until the bishop has blessed the boats.)

The parade was scheduled for a quarter after ten. It formed up in the parking lot by the wharf. At its center was a statue of St. Peter, carried in the bed of a pickup truck. It also included an honor guard from the V.F.W., the Women's Auxiliary of the V.F.W., the town crier, some men from the Knights of Columbus, two children's fife-and-drum bands—one from Connecticut and one from New Hampshire—the Provincetown Jug Band, and a marching band called the Taleb Grotto Band, from somewhere off the Cape. The Taleb Grotto Band was made up of members of a fraternal organization. They wore tasselled fezzes, and dinner jackets with a pattern of tiny gold roses. On their drum was the head of a Viking. Most of them appeared to be retired. They took each other's pictures while they waited, and talked about living in Florida. They had the kind, patient, uncertain, and polite-looking faces of elderly men who are not on their own turf. The Knights of Columbus wore black suits and red-and-black satin capes, and carried swords. The fife bands were dressed in Colonial outfits.

Jack appeared here and there in the crowd. He had already been to the waterfront, in the middle of the night. The police had called to say they had discovered the ropes on the banner above Commercial Street cut by someone who had been trying to steal it, and Jack had come down to secure it. A few moments before the parade was to get under way, Jack discovered that two of the boats tied up in front of the bishop's stand were not taking part in the blessing, and he ran off to call the harbormaster to arrange to have them moved. While he was gone, the Taleb Grotto

Band practiced a march and then retired to the shade to discuss whether the tempo had been right.

A man from the V.F.W. walked among the parade groups giving instructions for the order of the march. "The fishermen are going to walk right behind the second fife band," he said. "Whatever fishermen there is." There were ten of them, together with eight children. They marched with the statue of St. Peter, and they were the only group not to form ranks.

The parade was about a hundred yards long, and mainly red and white. It went up Commercial Street. The Taleb Grotto Band played "The Billboard" and the "DeMolay Commandery." The sun glinted on the bells of their horns. An old man in pajamas watched from behind a closed window. The parade passed clapboard houses with flower boxes, and houses with honeysuckle and trellised roses you could smell on the street. It passed a fence beside which stood two muscular men with oiled bodies who were holding up Chihuahuas. It passed Miss Pat's House of Beauty and Arnold's TV Service. It passed houses with boats in the yard and dogs tied up and cut hedges and yard statues. It passed a young man seated before a second story window, with his chin in his palm and half of his face in shadow.

At the church, people lined the walk crossing the lawn to the door. The Knights of Columbus drew their swords and took up positions along either side of it. Four fishermen shouldered the statue of St. Peter and carried it up the walk and up the stairs, into the church and down the aisle. The bishop followed. He wore red-and-white robes, and had a broad, open, handsome Irish face. His presence was comforting. He looked into the eyes of the people he passed on the walk and on the steps. His expression contained the pleasure and the benevolence one sometimes sees on the faces of Catholic officials who are out among the people on a day of celebration. Every seat in the church was taken. The congregation turned and watched the approach down the aisle of the statue, and followed it with their eyes to its place beside the altar. During the Mass, the bishop said prayers for the men lost at sea and for a bountiful catch and for the continued safe passage of the fishermen. The congregation received Communion. When the bishop said, "The Mass is ended. Go in peace to love and serve the Lord," the fishermen carried the statue back down the aisle and out the door, and the parade made a procession to the harbor.

The bishop was driven to the pier in a convertible. He climbed the steps to his place at the front of the stand. The wind blew his robes. He smiled a lot. He beamed. The two priests stood beside him, wearing sunglasses. Twenty-three boats, led by the Liberty, circled the harbor before him. Each boat carried forty or fifty guests. People straddled the gunwales and climbed the rigging and stood on the decks and on top of the pilothouses. The harbor within the breakwater was thronged with small boats. The Liberty threaded a path among them. Jill stood in the bow, holding a pine wreath. As the Liberty drew up to the pier, she threw the wreath into the water before the bishop looming above her.

The bishop held in his hand a shank of metal the length of a wrench and with a chamber at the end which he waved in the direction of the Liberty, and from which a few drops of holy water flew in an arc against the blue ground of the sky.

OVER the last ten years, the Provincetown fleet has lost four boats and the lives of fourteen fishermen. The Patricia Marie sank with seven men aboard in October, 1976; the Cap'n Bill sank with four men aboard in 1978; and the Victory II sank with three men aboard in 1984. (The Santina sank without loss of life.)

The Patricia Marie sank at night in a storm. She was heading to Provincetown with a deckful of scallops, and the scallops shifted suddenly with a wave and flipped her over. She was being followed into port at a distance of about a mile by another boat. The captains had talked over the radio, and were keeping a watch out for each other both on deck and by means of radar. The second boat rose to the top of a swell and saw the Patricia Marie's lights, then sank into the trough, and when it rose again the lights were gone. There was no longer an image representing her on the radar screen. The second boat arrived in ten minutes at the place where the Patricia Marie was last seen, and heard a voice calling for help. For another ten minutes, it made passes back and forth among the swells trying to pin down the voice in the dark, and then the voice fell silent. Among the seven men on board were a father and son, who made the second and third generations of their family lost at sea. A search was carried out, and the body of the captain was found, along with parts of the boat, but that was all, which is what the wife of one of the fishermen said she preferred. "It doesn't make sense for them to be taken out of the sea they loved so much. They belong together where they are."

The Cap'n Bill left the harbor on a Thursday in February and didn't come back. The men aboard were intending to fish for cod, and at that time of year they often made trips of two days. On Friday afternoon, the captain's wife drove out to the ocean to speak to her husband over the CB radio she had in her car, and was unable to raise him. She tried again on Friday evening, and again got no response, and told her stepson that she had a premonition of trouble. The two of them met the boats returning Saturday to see if any had word of the Cap'n Bill. No boat had seen her either on Friday or on Saturday, but one had seen her on Thursday evening, about four miles off the backshore of Truro, the town south of Provincetown. The weather on the days in between had been calm and clear. On Sunday morning, the captain's wife called the Coast Guard, which searched with planes and boats for several days over the ocean between Cape Ann and Nantucket and found nothing. Approximately a week and a half after the Cap'n Bill left port, another Provincetown captain caught his net in a place he had fished for twenty-eight years without ever having trouble. In trying to free himself, he brought to the surface a piece of a CB antenna, some freshly painted wood, and some oil. In order to mark the spot precisely, he remained where he was until the next day, when four divers arrived and descended the line attached to his net. Along the way, three of the divers had problems—the regulator on the air tank of one of them froze—and had to turn back. The one who made it to the bottom found a fishing boat in the darkness, beneath a hundred and thirty-seven feet of water, and was able to read the name by the light of a hand-held lamp. The lamp illuminated only the two feet within its narrow beam, and before the diver could make a complete search of the boat and discover whether the life raft was in its place he ran out of allotted air and had to ascend.

The boat had been found exactly where the captain's son had predicted it would be—on his father's favorite winter grounds, two and a half miles off the backshore of Truro. Two days later, all four divers made it to the bottom and completed the search. There were no bodies aboard, and the divers were unable to discover how the sinking had occurred. All they could tell, because the net was in place, was that the boat had been fishing when it happened. Ralph Andrews, the captain, was considered an uncommonly resourceful man. Not until the life raft was found intact aboard the sunken boat did his family give up hope.

The Victory II sank in the bay off Wellfleet, near Billingsgate Shoal. Her net caught on a cement anchor used to hold a Coast Guard buoy in place, and she rolled on her beam and sank quickly. She was discovered by a Wellfleet scalloper. She was under thirty-five feet of clear water, and the captain could see her plainly from his deck. The captain of the Victory II was Kenneth Macara, who was twenty-eight and a cousin of Jack's. A year later, parts of a skeleton came up in the nets of the Liberty Belle while she was fishing near Billingsgate. The Liberty Belle used to belong to one of Jack's uncles. In the week before the blessing the bones were identified as Kenneth Macara's.

# The Riverkeeper

THE HUDSON IS A COMPLICATED RIVER. IT contains salt, brackish, and fresh water, half of it is more properly an estuary than a river, it is tidal, and it flows in two directions. In places where it flows past cities—particularly where it flows past Albany and Troy and where it flows past New York—it is grotesquely polluted. People often think of it as a dead river. Nevertheless, the variety of life in the Hudson is greater now than it was when Verrazano discovered the river, in 1524. A number of species of fish have been introduced into the river, or into its tributaries and have found their way to the river, or have arrived in the river through the Erie Canal. A kind of sturgeon, the short-nosed sturgeon, which is endangered practically everywhere else, is plentiful in the Hudson. It is possible that there are as many as thirty million striped bass in the river. New York City occasionally takes a portion of its drinking water from the freshwater part of the river. Several towns along the river rely exclusively on the Hudson for their drinking supply, and for a number of years until recently fresh water was secretly taken from the Hudson and transported by tanker to Aruba, an arid island in the Caribbean. The bulk of it was put to industrial use, but at least one hotel used Hudson River water to fill its pool.

The river as it flows through New York Harbor is salty. Lobsters nest in the river. There are barnacles on the pilings in the harbor and oysters underneath the George Washington Bridge. The southernmost marsh on the river—Piermont Marsh, twenty miles north of the Statue of Liberty—is a saltwater marsh; saltwater plants grow in it, and saltwater creatures live in it. The Hudson turns brackish at Peekskill. The edge of the salt front fluctuates. Mainly, the tide and the current control it. Heavy rains drive it south, sometimes as far as the Battery. A dry summer advances it. The river is usually fresh above Newburgh, but in periods of drought the salt line occasionally extends to Poughkeepsie, seventy-five miles north of the Battery.

What accounts for the Hudson's being tidal is the riverbed's lying below sea level. The sea floods the river. The Hudson runs from the dam at Troy with no real change in elevation. The tide is about four and a half feet at the Battery, and about four and a half feet at Troy. The river at low tide looks especially unwholesome. People viewing its weedy, muddy, gull-bestrewn flats often think they are looking at the river in a drought. Tide is a measure of the rise and fall of water in the river. Current is the rate of progress of water through the bed of the river.

The relation of tide to current is not orderly. In places, the tide can be running along the banks and static in the channel; meanwhile, the river is flowing south. This makes the surface of the river look like herringbone. The current turns about two hours after the tide—that is, it takes about two hours for the column of water to slow to a stop in the face of the tide and reverse its direction. During heavy fall rains, the current sometimes runs south for nine and ten hours at a time. It is possible then to see a layer of fresh, clear water on the surface of the river. Because of the ebb and flow of the tide, the same water runs more than once past a fixed point on the river. Power plants, which draw river water for cooling, put the river in extra jeopardy, because the tide causes the same water to be swept more than once through the plant. In the water are the fry of spawning fish.

The surface of the river does not reveal depth; it is too silty for that. Its life is invisible. The colors on its surface are mainly a reflection of the sky. Under a uniform sky, the color of the water is consistent from bank to bank and up and down the river as far as you can see. Two feet of water looks the same in tone as twenty or sixty or eighty. It is sometimes possible to find the shallower parts by the appearance on the surface of long, stringy plants that grow up from the bottom. Sometimes these are out in the middle of the river, where you would expect there to be plenty of water. In the winter, it is easy to find shallows against the shore, because ice stacks up in them. The wind occasionally stirs up the bottom in the shallows and floats mud in solid streaks along the bank, which makes there appear to be two separate rivers. In bright light, the surface of the river is polished and shiny, like the finish of a car. It hurts your eyes to look at it. It almost blurs your vision.

On overcast days, it turns dark and gray and loses its luster, and is hardly reflective at all. Under a sky of scattered clouds, the river keeps changing color.

Sunlight penetrates approximately ten feet of the river and gives occasionally as much as six inches' visibility, but deeper than that there is none. Fish swim in the dark. Police Department divers working in the river often close their eyes and use their hands to locate objects, or hope to bump into them, because it gives them a headache to try and focus in the gloom. On the bottom of the river are wrecks, as well as every possible kind of trash, as well as rocks and mud and silt and sludge, as well as tools and steel girders that have fallen off bridges under construction. At Newburgh, parts of the bottom of the river are paved to a depth of about a foot with beer bottles. On the bottom of portions of the part of the river that passes the city are lengths of unspooled movie film, and no one knows why. Occasionally, Police Department divers get tangled up in it. Sometimes they swim into phone booths.

Many American rivers are larger than the Hudson: the Alabama, the Apalachicola-Chattahoochee, the Assiniboine, the Black, the Big Black, the Brazos, the Cedar, the Churchill, the Connecticut, the Coppermine, the Cumberland, the Delaware, the Fraser, the Gila, the James, the Kanawha-New, the Koyukuk, the Mackenzie, the Milk, the Mississippi, the Neosho, the Osage, the Ouachita, the Peace, the Pearl, the Pecos, the Pend Oreille, the Platte, the Powder, the Republican, the Sabine, the Savannah, the Snake, the Tanana, the Tombigbee, the White, and the Yukon. Plus almost sixty others. The Hudson is three hundred and fifteen miles long, and narrow in many places, but if you are standing on the shore at Stony Point and staring the three and a half miles across Haverstraw Bay it looks as if it must be the biggest river in the world.

.  .  .

A HUNDRED and eighty-six species of fish are found in
the river, of which seventy-three are saltwater fish. Five
kinds of fish use the river: freshwater fish such as large-
and smallmouth bass; fish such as the American eel, which
live in fresh water but spawn at sea; saltwater fish such as
bluefish, which during the first year of their lives move
inshore to feed; saltwater fish such as shad and striped
bass, which spawn in fresh water; and estuarine fish—that
is, saltwater fish such as hogchokers (a kind of small sole)
and bay anchovies, which spend their lives mainly in
water of low salt content. Exotic fish stray into the river
while migrating or are blown off course by storms. Some
arrive following warm water. The Gulf Stream doglegs
east off New York Harbor; eddies wheel off it and close
up like soap bubbles and drift into the river. If the fish
within them survive the winter, it is usually by locating
a discharge of heated water from a power plant. Fishermen on the river whose main interest is in catching exotic fish pay special attention to the outflows of power
plants. Warm-water strays such as lookdowns, spots,
mullets, ladyfish, mangrove snappers, fat sleepers, jack
crevalles, northern stargazers, orange filefish, Atlantic
needlefish, and flying gurnards turn up in nets, and are
sometimes caught from the shore. Practically any creature
that lives in the ocean can wander into the river. Not
long ago, a whale swam up the river as far as Forty-
second Street. In 1936, a school of dolphins swam nearly
to Albany. Seals visit the river. One lived several months
in the river the year before last. A man watched it floating on its back and eating a catfish. Another man took
pictures of it sunning itself on a dock. Recently, a member

of the New York City police diving team saw a sea turtle floating in the river. The policeman said it looked like a hubcap.

The striped bass in the river are believed to be divided among four populations. Three are transient. Two of these are believed to winter in the river and leave after spawning in the spring. The third enters the Hudson only to spawn. The fourth is thought to be resident. The resident bass have orange stripes and are called strawberry bass. In winter, striped bass collect beneath the ice of Haverstraw Bay and the Tappan Zee. They gather in enormous schools and lie relatively still and close to the bottom in from twenty-five to forty feet of water. As the river warms in the spring, the slumbering bass spread into the shallows to feed. Off Ossining, and by Croton Point, and off a place called Georges Island are old oyster beds and shoals where striped bass gather. South of Verplanck is a bed of oyster shells about two miles long and half a mile wide. The bed is dense and tightly packed, and an anchor dropped there will slide right along the bottom as if there were cement down there, as if it had been dropped in a swimming pool. At the edge of this bed, stripers feed. Striped bass caught in the part of the river that flows past the city taste of kerosene. The people who fish for them—Hispanic people, mainly—marinate them a day or so in lemon juice before cooking them.

THE pollution in the river is both chemical and bacterial. The bacteria consume oxygen, especially during hot weather, and in places where they are extraordinarily abundant they use up so much of it that the water stagnates and the fish among them drown. Scores of chemicals of varying toxicity are dumped into the river each year, some with permits from the New York State Department of Environmental Conservation and some secretly. Some companies receive permits for discharges into the river, and comply with their provisions; some companies either forgo permits entirely and dump mainly at night or receive a permit for a certain chemical or a certain number of discharges and then improvise. The main chemical menace to the river is the hundreds of thousands of pounds of polychlorinated-biphenyl compounds, known as PCBs, dumped into it over a period of years by the General Electric Company from its factories at Hudson Falls and Fort Edward. General Electric began dumping PCBs into the river in 1945. In 1972, the passage of the Clean Water Act made it necessary for the company to have a permit, which it was recommended for by the D.E.C. and awarded by the E.P.A. In 1975, it was announced that PCBs had been found in the tissues of fish in the river. Some of the highest amounts were found in eels. PCBs collect in fat tissues, and of the fish in the river eels have the most fat. In 1976, the taking of eels from the river was prohibited, and so was commercial fishing for striped bass. The Department of Health recommended that people eat no more than half a pound a month of striped bass from the river, and of other fish in the river none at all, and that women of child-bearing age and children under fifteen eat no fish from the river. The Food and Drug Administration believes that more than two parts per million of PCBs in a fish is a hazard; Hudson River striped bass average between four and five parts per million, and have for a number of years. (During the nineteen-seventies, striped bass measuring more than fifty parts per million were found in the Hudson.) A striped bass caught anywhere else in New York state is a fish that has probably spent some part of its year in the Hudson. In 1985, because of PCB contamination from the Hudson, commercial fishing for striped bass was banned in New York state, except off eastern Long Island, and in 1986 recreational fishing for striped bass was banned. In addition, the commercial ban became total. For a year, the possession of a striped bass from New York water was illegal. Along the river, the ban was ignored and unenforced and difficult to defend: striped bass were by no means the most heavily contaminated fish in the river.

PCBs settle to the bottom. Areas where there are concentrations of at least fifty parts per million are called hot spots. It is believed that there are approximately two hundred thousand pounds of PCBs in hot spots above the Troy dam and a hundred and seventy-seven thousand pounds dispersed throughout the upper river. A hundred and fifty thousand pounds are thought to have travelled over the dam and dispersed themselves throughout the estuary. In 1976, G.E. paid a settlement of three million dollars and stopped dumping PCBs into the river. In addition, it donated a million dollars for research on the river. The D.E.C. paid a settlement of three million dollars for improper regulatory practices. Removing the hot spots from the river will cost approximately eighty million dollars.

During the years when the ban was only on fish in the river, commercial fishermen found hard to swallow the idea that the river could be swarming with striped bass and they couldn't touch them but as soon as the fish left the river someone else could. The definition of the boundaries of the river became exquisitely precise. Pinhookers—men who fish commercially with hook and line—would wait in the fall for striped bass leaving the river. They would wait in the harbor by the Statue of Liberty, and they would wait in Hell Gate, off the upper East Side, and they would wait in the East River off LaGuardia Airport. Some fishermen upriver would drift-net at night and sell their bass without saying where the catch came from. Among the fishermen, these fish were called bootleg bass. When the first ban on fishing was imposed, fish prices were high, and many fishermen on the river had bought new equipment with the idea of quitting their regular jobs and fishing full time. Eels were the river's staple fish. The fishermen had stacks of eel pots, they were ready to go.

PROFESSIONAL responsibility and personal obsession meet on the river in John Cronin. John works for the Hudson River Fishermen's Association, patrolling the estuary in a boat the association had built for him. The estuary is a hundred and fifty-four miles long. The Fishermen's Association has never told him what to do. He has no job description. He has no plan. He watches the river. He searches for places where towns or factories are dumping things into it without permission, or trying to fill it or bury beside it chemicals that might seep into it. He follows the runs of spawning fish. By towing a trawl in one part of the river, he learns what is living there, and by trawling again a week later he discovers what replaces it in the schedule of the river's migrations. On occasion, he commits sections of the shoreline to memory. He believes that it is important for someone to have the entire picture of it in his head. John's title is riverkeeper. He is the only person in America who lists "riverkeeper" as his occupation on his tax forms.

The idea of having a riverkeeper was suggested by Robert H. Boyle, the president of the Fishermen's Association. Boyle is in his late fifties. He is small and ardent and tenacious. I once asked him where the shad that spawn in the Hudson spend the rest of the year, and by the end of the explanation he had pulled from his bookshelves and spread out on a desk and read aloud from nautical charts of the river, road maps of Maine and Nova Scotia, three books on crustaceans, a volume of the *Canadian Journal of Fisheries and Aquatic Sciences,* a copy of "Keys to Marine Invertebrates of the Woods Hole Region," manila folders containing newspaper and magazine articles on shad (several of which he had written), a copy of the book "Anglers' Guide to the United States Atlantic Coast," a pamphlet entitled "Guide to Angling for Hudson River Shad," a copy of "A Historical Review of the Shad Fisheries of North America," a copy of *The Angler's Guide Book and Tourists' Gazetteer of the Fishing Waters of the United States and Canada* for the year 1885, several university studies on shad spawning and migration, and a copy of "McClane's New Standard Fishing Encyclopedia." There are people who know more than Boyle does about specific parts of the river or specific things having to do with its life—he is not a naturalist, and he is not a scientist—but I don't think there is anyone whose knowledge of the Hudson is more comprehensive. Much of what he knows he has published in a book called "The Hudson River," which appeared in 1969 and is still in print.

The idea for the job came to him when he read "River Keeper," by J. W. Hills. "River Keeper," published in 1934, is a portrait of William Lunn, who for almost fifty years was keeper of a private stretch of trout water on the Test, in England. Lunn's duties were to prevent poaching, to hatch and raise trout, to remove mud, to preserve an unimpeded flow of water, to destroy "vermin and pike and other coarse fish," to encourage the breeding of fly, and especially to see that the weeds along the banks in which fly naturally breed were cared for properly. On an inner leaf of his copy of the book Boyle has written, "A River-keeper must be put on the Hudson—and other American rivers—in the public interest." The money to equip a riverkeeper and support him at an adequate salary came in 1980, from a suit the Fishermen's Association brought against Con Edison and other utilities over fish kills at power plants. In addition, the association applied money received from the settlement of a suit it had brought with others against Con Edison to prevent the utility from building a power plant on the river at Storm King Mountain. John Cronin is not the first riverkeeper on the Hudson. The first was Tom Whyatt. He held the job for two and a half years, beginning in the summer of 1973. He used his own canoe to patrol the river, and the Fishermen's Association paid him a hundred dollars a week, from which he was able to save, after expenses, thirty-five dollars a week. He left because he could no longer afford to stay, and now works for an environmental organization in New York City.

The boat that John pilots is twenty-five feet long and is also called Riverkeeper. The name is written on both sides of the hull and is as visible from a distance as the writing on a billboard. The boat's hull is painted white, and its details are red and blue. It has a small cabin, where a person can stand crouching, and it has two bunks. It was built in a yard at Kingston. It is beamy and shallow-drafted, so there is almost nowhere on the river it cannot go; its hull is light, which makes it easy to beach; and its engine sits in a well several feet forward of the stern, so that it can haul nets without having them catch in the propeller. John is extremely careful with the boat. Many events of significance can be overlooked or forgotten by John if they have taken place aboard the boat on a day it receives a dent.

John lives beside the river, at Garrison. His house is on a strip of land separated from the marsh behind it by the bed of the railroad. The marsh is a cattail marsh, called Manitou Marsh, and it is artificial, in the sense that it did not exist until the railroad cut it off from the rest of the river. It is full of songbirds—song sparrows, swamp sparrows, marsh wrens, and blackbirds. Beyond it are hills. The tracks of the railroad are slightly elevated; the passing trains loom above a person standing in John's driveway. They appear to ride at an angle, leaning out, and look as if they could easily tip over. John's dog chases them. The trains blow their whistles as they round the curve just south of his house, and the dog howls. The people who live on this strip of land call the southern half, which is uninhabited, the island. On the northern half there are sixteen houses, all of them built close together, all of them frame, none of them especially old, and all of them different in design. John's house has two small bedrooms and a living room with a picture window overlooking a back yard that runs about thirty-five feet to the river. The yard has a nautical theme; in it are a couple of fishing nets, some buoys, and a flat-bottomed Hudson River shad boat that John built with a friend and used on the river. From the edge of John's yard to the opposite bank is approximately half a mile. On the far bank are hills with houses on top of them. At night, the river reflects their lights.

When the former owner of John's house decided to sell the place, he put up a "For Sale" sign on the lawn facing the water, and John saw it from the river. From the river the houses look like toy houses beside a model-railroad track. The throb of the engines of the freight trains on the opposite bank and of the freighters and tankers passing on the river resonates against the hills and the water and makes the windows in John's house vibrate. His tap draws water from the river, but he does not drink it. He buys his drinking water at the supermarket. Sometimes he moors the boat at Cold Spring and sometimes at his house. Off the lawn is a mooring for the boat. He is able to park the boat as close to his house as most suburban people are able to park their cars. He says that one of his favorite things about his job is driving home in a boat.

John is thirty-six years old. He has blue eyes and blond hair. He is about six feet tall. His head is large and his face is full, which makes him seem heavier than he is. He is lanky and loose-jointed. His shoulders are narrow. He has a habit of thrusting his chin forward when he speaks, so that he looks like a man trying to free his neck of a tight collar, or like a man tossing in his sleep. In conversation, he has a tendency to withdraw his interest, sometimes abruptly, which makes him appear to be restless and impatient. He is occasionally remote. A person talking to him often feels that his attention is somewhere else. If you ask him a question, you sometimes have to repeat it. His eyes move around a lot when he talks. He is often staring into the distance. He is very comfortable by himself and spends a lot of time alone. He does not always keep regular hours. He is persistent and unself-conscious in pursuing a piece of information he feels is being withheld from him. He will stand in front of a person who does not give him the answer he wants and stare off and not say a word, until the person grows uncomfortable enough to give in. Newspaper articles about him like to mention that he did not learn how to operate a boat until he was thirty.

His form at the wheel of the Riverkeeper, racing across the river with the wind blowing his hair, is attractive to newspapers and magazines and television crews and filmmakers. When he has to spend the day with a television crew, he usually busies himself with small errands around the boat until one of them comes up to him and says, "I have a great idea for a shot. We'll get you racing across the river, as if you'd just been called to an emergency." If he feels that they are taking too long to come up with it, he will sometimes suggest the idea himself.

A man from Hollywood has approached him with the idea of making a movie for television about his life on the river. In a nightmare he sometimes has, he is a character in the movie. So is the boat. The boat can talk.

John has his office in a shingle-sided two-story farmhouse on the grounds of an estate in Garrison. The house stands at the foot of high hills, about half a mile from the river. All around it are fields. From its porch you can see the hills on the opposite bank. Tall trees edge the winding gravel drive. In summer, from the fields, there is a constant sound of crickets. In addition to John, the Fishermen's Association employs a fundraiser, a secretary, a researcher, and a lawyer, who has an office upstairs in the farmhouse. The lawyer likes to dive in the river with aqualungs. For a while, whenever he found an exotic fish or one of unusual size he would capture it and bring it back to the farmhouse and put it in the freezer compartment of the refrigerator in the kitchen. The lawyer went diving a lot. Pretty soon the freezer was full. The door had to be opened carefully. Otherwise, the fish would come sliding out, and it would sound as if someone had dropped blocks of wood on the floor. After a while, John felt there were a sufficient number of samples in the freezer and asked him not to collect any more.

On the walls of John's office are maps of the river, some framed illustrations of fish, some books, and a picture of John on the boat racing across the river with the wind blowing his hair, as if he were on his way to an emergency. The most prominent object in the office is an immense fish tank filled with creatures from the river and its tributaries. Some of the things in the tank were caught by the lawyer, and some of them came up in trawls that John made for one reason or another from the boat. There is a small blue crab, there are freshwater mussels from the Wallkill, there is a pickerel and a largemouth bass, there are a number of hogchokers, and there are catfish and sunnies and suckers and eels. For a while, there was a crayfish, but it molted and something ate it before it found cover. John keeps its shell on his desk. In warm weather, the fish in the tank are fed minnows seined from the river. In cold, they get goldfish from a pet store. The tank is suffused with anxiety. Everything in it is permanently on guard against everything else—mainly the bass and the pickerel. The pickerel bit the lawyer's finger once and drew blood. The rest of the inhabitants are either hiding, or ambushing one another, or burying themselves and killing time until dark, when it is safer to come out. Sometimes the larger fish follow movement in the room with their eyes. When they get hungry, they line up at the glass and stare out without moving.

On top of a filing cabinet beside John's desk is a postcard from the Caribbean. It shows three dories, painted red-white-and-blue, and a powerboat, painted yellow, moored in a cove. The water is acutely blue. Beyond is a white beach, and in the distance several dozen smokestacks poke up like stubble in a cornfield. On the back of the card the stacks are identified: "Lago Oil Refinery: one of the world's largest, most modern, and cleanest refinery and desulphurization plants. Aruba—Neth. Antilles." The plant ran for many years using Hudson River water. John has never seen the refinery, but he knows a lot about it.

The card, from a friend, is a kind of souvenir of his biggest case so far. When John had been on the water about a month, he learned that the Exxon Corporation was taking fresh water from the Hudson without permission and transporting it by tanker to Aruba. In settling the suit, Exxon paid the Fishermen's Association half a million dollars. John would love to find another deep pocket like that for the river.

USUALLY, when I visit John I take the train to Garrison Landing, fifty miles from the city. The tracks of the railroad follow the river almost all the way. I have made the trip often enough that I know where to look for his house. Sometimes, through the branches of the trees I can see the boat moored off his yard. Sometimes I see his dog running alongside the tracks. I have made the trip at all times of year, but I prefer it during the winter, when the river is carrying ice. There is hardly any traffic on it then, and you can look at it in a way you can't when there are sailboats all over it. Once, from the window of a train I saw a dog drifting downriver on a sheet of ice. Another time, I saw a deer on an ice floe. It was out near the middle of the channel, and it was facing the opposite shore, and it turned and watched the train over its shoulder. It looked like an animal on a broad, empty plain. I like especially to be passing in the evening between North Tarrytown and Scarborough. The river there is about two miles wide. On the far bank are hills, behind which the sun sets, turning the sky the colors of a simple household fire.

I have been aboard the Riverkeeper on a day in October when John was taking Bob Boyle out fishing off Con Hook Reef, south of Cold Spring, and then off Fish Island, a small prominence of rock just south of the reef, to see what was there on the change of the tide. I have been out with him on a day in the spring when there were rows of cormorants along the bank stretching their wings to dry in the sun. Some of them took to the air when they saw us. Cormorants are black and have long necks and small heads. They are related to pelicans, and they can swim underwater. In flight, making their gradual, almost horizontal rise into the air, they look like bowling pins with wings. I have been with him on a windy day in October when we could follow the progress of clouds across the sky by their shadows on the surface of the river. I have been with him also on a cool day in October when, hoping to find butterfish for the American Museum of Natural History, he and Tom Lake, an officer of the Fishermen's Association, made five trawls in Haverstraw Bay and collected about a thousand fish—mainly striped bass and bluefish and white perch and bay anchovies and hogchokers—but struck out on butterfish. I have been with him on a day in November when the sky was so clear that we could see the outline of buildings in New York City from the Tappan Zee. I went out with him one evening in December to look at a cove that is so choked in the summer with water chestnuts that he can't get the boat into it, and we came home in the dark, and it was really cold, and the water was so smooth that the sensation of crossing it was almost like flying. I have been with him on hot, hazy days when the river is gray and the sky is white and the hills in the distance are blue. I made a trip with him one spring day from Cold Spring to Catskill Creek—sixty miles. In Poughkeepsie, we stopped and watched police divers haul the body of a drowned man from the river. We spent the night in a slip at Hop-O-Nose Marine, on Catskill Creek. Herring jumped all night in the creek. It sounded like someone spooning water from a basin with his hands. In the morning, tree swallows hunted the river. Two fishermen set drift nets. They wore yellow slickers and stood in their boat facing each other with their heads bent, paying out net across the channel. Theirs was the only other boat on the river. On the far bank, a deer came out of the woods, crossed the railroad tracks, dived into the water, swam toward the channel, saw the fishermen in the boat, turned around, swam back, trotted out of the water, shook itself like a dog, then loped across the tracks and disappeared into the woods. An osprey dived between two ducks, hitting the water hard and scaring up the ducks. Five men stood watching a sixth work a scap net for herring, off an oil-storage yard. The fisherman had a string in his hand, and at its other end was a live herring, tied through its mouth and its gills. The man was leading the herring back and forth in the water above the net. When a sufficient number of herring had joined the decoy, he raised the net quickly. A herring used this way is called a Judas herring.

That day, from the river, we watched fishermen haul-seining shad off Greendale Dock, a landing opposite Catskill. The men and women working the seines were collecting fish for two clients: a scientist from Canada tagging shad as a means of determining how many pass through the Bay of Fundy on migrations, and a group from Pennsylvania collecting shad by permission of New York State in the hope of restoring the run in the Susquehanna River. The Susquehanna-bound fish were to be loaded aboard tank trucks; through the branches of trees on the shore we could see the trucks parked beside the railroad tracks. The Pennsylvania people had hoped for six thousand fish, but had appeared late in the season and were not certain to get them. It had been determined by computer that the shad would arrive around the beginning of May; instead, they were in the river by the fifteenth of April. The fishermen hired to collect the fish thought it was hilarious that scientists had tried to predict the arrival of fish by computer.

The setting and retrieval of the net took about thirty minutes. In the first haul, there were plenty of herring but only six shad. For the benefit of a photographer, one of the seiners pulled a catfish from the net and held it high above his head with both hands, then flipped it up and behind him. It hung for a moment in the air like a game fish, then fell back to the river, looking as its image grew dimmer in the silty water as if it were dissolving.

JOHN SPEAKING: "The explanation of how I got to where I am is circuitous. I will try to tell it as briefly as possible. I was born in Yonkers, New York, the next town upriver from the Bronx, in July of 1950. I have a younger sister, who lives with her husband and son and daughter in Yonkers next door to my parents, and a younger brother, who lives in England and has started his own zoo. My father, who must have been about twenty-six when I arrived, worked for the Otis Elevator Company. Within a few years, he packed up my mother and my brother and me and moved us to Baltimore. The grass was greener. He was restless, and I have always had a feeling that I carry with me his idea of constantly moving to something better—even just something else. In Baltimore, he worked selling ice-cream franchises. Two years of watching people put their life savings into ice-cream stores and watching them fail. I remember clearly the school I went to, but I have no special feelings for Baltimore. It was hard to make friends. They weren't big on Northerners—and anyway we moved three times. My father had a strategy for getting the kids to play with me and my brother. He held little events. Warm evenings, he would show movies outdoors in the yard against the wall of our apartment building. Got popcorn, and all the kids would come and throw things and spill drinks and have a great time, and the next day in school they wouldn't talk to us.

"When we returned to Yonkers, my father resumed work at the Otis Elevator Company, but without his seniority. I don't think he went back to his old job. I think he went back to the job before that. He had begun as a time-study man. Time-study man is the one whose job it is to determine how long it should take to complete a given task. It was not a laborer's job, and it had a kind of title, but he made less than the machinists. Over the years, he worked his way up slowly through the company. What he wanted, of course, was an executive's position. What he arrived at eventually was personnel manager. Otis was pretty much a turn-of-the-century industry—huge machines, and numbing amounts of noise, and sunlight filtering through a constant veil of dust. At times, in certain parts of the factory, you could barely see your hand in front of your face.

"By the time my parents got their present home, when I was fourteen, I had lived in seven different places with them. Always renting. We were endlessly looking for a home. A family outing on a Sunday would be for my father to drive my brother and my sister and my mother and me to these neighborhoods where people owned their homes. Then we would walk through the rooms and attics of the houses that were for sale, opening the doors of the closets and staring out the windows. My recollection is that we did this for years—the reason being no money, I guess. I think that my parents were always looking for a house that would make them do something irresponsible. Like buy it.

"The house they finally bought was not grand. It did not, for example, include a bedroom for me. My father worked an extra job evenings. He worked at a Thom McAn shoe store for a while, he sold sporting goods, he worked behind the counter of a deli. Borrowed from Peter to pay Paul. 'How'd you pay for the house, Dad?' 'Borrowed from Peter to pay Paul.' Every evening, I fell asleep in my parents' bed, and sometime during the night my father would return and, without disturbing me, move me to the bed in the living room, where in the morning I would wake up. That I did not have a room of my own did not seem unusual to me.

"In addition to a home's being special, an idea that is important in my family is work. My parents took it for granted that I would work as soon as I could. Salesboy, soda jerk, paperboy—something. I began working summers at Otis when I was fourteen; we lied about my age. I worked one summer sweeping floors, another counting nuts and bolts. A third I spent in the stifling heat of the foundry. My father expected all of us to believe in the importance of a college education, which neither my brother nor I ever got. The irony is that throughout our childhood it never occurred to us that our father was not a powerful figure at the Otis Elevator Company. We saw what he had accomplished in the world without the benefit of a college education, and had no thought or ambition to surpass him. We thought it was enough.

"After high school, I moved to Hartford, Connecticut, and went—I should say tried to go—to the University of Hartford, but the attempt lasted only two semesters. At some point during my freshman year, I decided I wanted to be a dancer. I don't know where that came from, really.

It's a mystery to me. All I can think of is that I remember home movies of my mother and father in a minstrel show and that I used to love watching them. At the university, I began taking modern-dance classes in the fall, out of interest, and then I came to New York over Christmas and took part for a week in a seminar given by Martha Graham. When I went back to Connecticut, I tried out for a scholarship to the Hartford Ballet School, and I got it. So, instead of college, for the rest of the winter and most of the spring I went to ballet school. I showed up at the college for classes once in a while, but mostly I was dancing. Not with devotion, especially—with mixed feelings. But I was doing it.

"One day that spring, I was driving home in a car with some friends. The top was down, and we were on a road I didn't know, and the sky was very clear, and I was laying my head back, watching it, as we drove, and all of a sudden my ambivalence disappeared. My thoughts went like this: I'm in a car, it's a beautiful day, I have to quit school. A moment of clarity.

"I decided to see the country. I quit dancing. To raise money for my trip, I took a job in the Catskills leading people on trail rides. I didn't know anything about horses, and I couldn't believe how big they were. My girlfriend and I left New York in February, travelling with three other people, three cats, and a dog in a Plymouth Valiant sedan. Destination Phoenix. Two of the people had been to Arizona, and it was winter, and we just wanted to be someplace warm.

"We went first to New Mexico, and arrived during a blizzard. Santa Fe. The place was shut down from the cold. No electricity. No gas in people's houses. No power. We crept through the country in this cold, cold time.

Driving through a pass outside of town, I watched the
temperature gauge on my car dropping as we climbed
higher and higher, and I thought, Is it possible that my
car can freeze while I am driving it?

"In Arizona, I washed dishes at a Howard Johnson's.
We stayed several months and felt the heat coming on and
moved to Boulder, Colorado. The first night there, we
slept in the car with the cats and all our possessions and
got arrested. Afterward, we drove in to town to buy groceries and had an accident in the supermarket parking lot—
a guy crippled my radiator. Which means he's just put a
dent in my house. Which means he's just wrecked my
house. I called a tow truck, and a man arrived and loaded
up my car and told me I could come and work on it next
day at his junk yard, he wouldn't charge me. I tell him,
Well, fine, but it's where I live, and he looks up at the sky
a moment and then back down at us and says all right,
we can sleep in it there, too. We decided first to go into
Boulder and see if we couldn't find a place from talking
to someone on the street—which is what every second
person was doing anyway. No luck, and eventually it
grew dark. We gave the cats away and set out for the junk
yard, which was three or four miles across town, and on
the way it rained, and then a carload of townies passed by
and pelted us with eggs. When we reached the junk yard,
we saw the car on the hook. The guy hadn't taken it off
the hook. Can't sleep there. So we poked around the junk
yard, and there was a dog howling somewhere, and it was
pitch black and rainy, and we found an old Volkswagen
bus with the sunroof off, which hadn't been crushed so
badly that it had lost its shape, and we found a wooden
door and stretched it between the seats for a mattress, and
lay down and drew a sheet of plastic over us. It was a low

point, but self-imposed. All from a moment of clarity. I live now, at thirty-six, somewhat in fear of another moment of clarity.

"I sacked groceries in Boulder. Washing dishes was better. Then I became a salesman of books door to door in South Bend, Indiana. I signed up with a recruiter in Boulder and went to sales school in Nashville, Tennessee. School lasted five days. Selling is a religion down South—something they do with real fervor. They preached to us about it. They gave us little books and pamphlets to study: 'The Greatest Salesman in the World,' by Og Mandino. They created an imaginary prospect and called her Mrs. Jones and equipped us with a sales talk for her. Her children are at school, her husband is away at his job, and she is going to be delighted to see us. 'And what are you going to say to Mrs. Jones?' That kind of thing. Call and response. You go up the steps and you knock on the door—never ring the bell, knocking is more personal, it makes them curious, especially if they have a bell—then turn your back, and when Mrs. Jones comes to the door she has to say something first. What I represented was an enormous book, like ten textbooks rolled into one, called The Volume Library. I had a bicycle to sell with. Everyone in South Bend is Catholic, and every street is Knute Rockne Boulevard, or Knute Rockne Avenue, or Knute Rockne Drive. Every home I managed to get into had a child in the corner with jelly on its diaper. One of my partners made a fortune taking deposits from people he knew wouldn't be able to make payment on delivery—it was a nonrefundable deposit. I had no particular success, and didn't feel comfortable in the Midwest anyway, and when it was over I moved back to Boulder. The guy subletting my apartment had talked the landlord into giving it to him. I stayed with friends for a while.

"When I moved back to New York, it was to the Hudson Valley. I worked, successively, as a carpenter, a roofer, a roofing salesman, and a bouncer. Then there was a period of working around the river—working nearby and on things to do with the river—and then I fell into working on the river itself, and when I did, it was complete, like quitting school. I was first a volunteer for the sloop Clearwater. Then I joined its staff for a project called Clearwater Pipewatch. This was the first investigative work I did. The project was organized by Tom Whyatt, the original riverkeeper. We used to go right out to the company premises and find the discharges into the river and its tributaries and sample them. It produced information that led to the investigation of several companies, one of which was the Tuck tape company, in Beacon. It had a permit for two discharges but really made twenty-nine. The guy from the company called me a Boy Scout with binoculars. I worked on Pipewatch for three years, and then I took a job with an organization called the Center for the Hudson River Valley. I was a lobbyist and environmental director, and I worked on three pretty important pieces of state legislation: the Hudson River Fishery Management Program, which was intended to develop a strategy for reviving Hudson River fishing; the Hudson River Shorelands Preservation Act; and the New York Coastal Erosion Hazard Areas Act. From working with them I decided I wanted to learn more about government, so I took a job with Congressman Hamilton Fish. For Congressman Fish I was a district coördinator, which meant that it was my job to be a liaison to businesses, local governments, public groups, and labor unions for the purpose of explaining federal projects and federal issues. Following that, I worked for the chairman of the New York State Assembly Committee on Environmental

Conservation. There I helped draft environmental legislation and also did work on the Love Canal and on the toxic-waste-dumping practices of the Army in New York state.

"In a little while, I fell under the influence of a man named Bob Gabrielson, a commercial fisherman in Nyack. It was extremely important for me that I met him when I did. I stole time here and there to work with him for two seasons. Then, in the third, which was 1981, I gave up my apartment and moved into my truck and lived in the back of it, parked on his dock."

BOB GABRIELSON has the use of a point of land on the river off Burd Street in Nyack, just above the Tappan Zee Bridge. He has been there for many years. There is a boat club next door. He sets nets for shad in the spring and then traps for crabs through the summer, just north of the bridge. He has a road-paving business, mostly driveways, on which he spends the rest of the year, and he also works a sideline in tax preparation. Beside the river he has a flat-roofed, plank-floored plywood shanty, about seven feet by twelve. Facing the river is a window covered with plastic. There are dried fish scales all over the floor, like little chips of mica; there are two bunks, with blankets but no mattresses; there is a locker for staples and nails and cleats and spare parts; there are kerosene lanterns hanging on nails in the wall, beside life preservers and fishing rods; there is an old, battered, threadbare armchair, a plank bench, and the kind of market scale that has a basket, for weighing fish; there is a coffeemaker; there is a clothesline, for drying coats and gloves, stretched between two chairs above a small gas heater; and there are layers and layers of sweatshirts and foul-weather gear heaped on hooks and piled up all over the floor. During shad season, there are usually a number of fishermen in the shanty, sorting through the clothes and talking about which nets the fish are hitting, whether inside or out, and planning so that the men who work fastest take the nets that have the most fish. While they talk, they struggle into foul-weather gear, because early in the shad season it can get pretty cold.

A day shad fishing is really two days, because the fishermen work the flood tides, which occur every twelve hours. They fish and eat and sleep, and rise and fish and eat and sleep. The tides advance an hour each day, so that one day they fish at six and six and the next at seven and seven. Occasionally, the fish show up in such numbers that the fishermen have to keep on the nets, which means working both flood and ebb tides. There are six weeks of fishing to the season, and by the time it plays out and the weather turns warm many of the fishermen are glad to see it go.

Gabrielson uses nets of two hundred feet. The nets are strung about eighteen inches below the surface, so that the driftwood and the trash of the river can clear them. They have a mesh of five and a half inches, which allows small fish like herring to pass; they are made of monofilament; and they are cheaper to replace than to mend. The monofilament is of a gauge as fine as possible, because fish can sense a net if the twine is too heavy, and a whole school will detour around one. The nets are set in a line perpendicular to the shore, and traditionally, on the river, the stakes they are strung between are of shagbark hickory, but Gabrielson uses ash, which he gathers from the hills around Nyack. When he hears that a developer is clearing ground, he asks if he can take the ash from it, and guarantees the developer shad in return. The nets are from ten feet to twelve feet deep. The channel falls off gradually on the Nyack side of the river, which is the western side, and dramatically on the other. Gabrielson's nets reach from the middle of the river to the channel. Shad are a channel-run fish, so more of them escape than are caught. Upriver, the fishermen drift-net for shad in the channel, but their nets are much smaller. A fisherman's nets must come out of the water at six Friday morning and can go back at six on Saturday night. This is called the lift period, and it is enforced by the D.E.C.

Each boat is worked by two men. Once the nets have been set, one man operates the boat, and the other sits at the point of the bow, facing the stern, and pulls the net across the bow and over his lap. The fish come aboard with the net and are untangled from it and tossed into boxes. The net goes immediately back into the river. The boat works its way across the two hundred feet, from one pole to the next, and how long it takes depends on how many fish are in the net and how skilled the fishermen happen to be at their trade. Gabrielson's nets are right next to the bridge, and a person hauling them can hear the traffic and see the faces of the drivers of the cars on the bridge.

The fish are sorted and iced on the dock. Gabrielson has a truck bed beside the shanty which he uses as a cooler if he is keeping them overnight before sending them to the market. There are three major runs of shad—forsythia, lilac, and dogwood, which correspond to the appearance of those blooms on the shore. The bloom of the forsythia announces the arrival of shad in the river. Some time ago, Gabrielson went to a tree nursery and bought a forsythia bush and planted it in his yard, to let him know about the shad. Lilac shad are the climax of the run and are bigger. The forsythia run generally includes more buck shad, and the dogwood run more roe. The flesh of the buck is firmer

and tastes better but is worth next to nothing. The roe—
that is, the eggs—are what makes the fish valuable. Buck
shad are sold mainly to lobstermen on the Connecticut
shore, who use them as bait.

Gabrielson is close to six feet, but portly, so he doesn't
look as tall as he is. He has fished almost every year on
the river since he was twelve years old, and he is now
fifty-seven. He has gray hair and a wide, round face and
practically always wears a billed cap, and glasses, and on
the water he smokes a cigar. He is extremely happy whenever he is out on the river—it doesn't even have to be an
especially nice day—and, sitting at the wheel of his boat
with his cigar and looking out at his nets, he will suddenly
turn to you and say, "Where the hell would you rather be
in your life than out on this river?"

Following shad season, Gabrielson crabs. He strings a
trap every fifty feet along four hundred and fifty feet of
line. He generally sets ten lines. He baits the traps with
menhaden or white perch seined from the river, and
weights the traps so that they sit bottom down. He doesn't
mark their placement with a float, because that would be
an advertisement to poachers. The line suspends itself out
of sight beneath the surface of the river. He locates the
general area by coördinates on the shore—a dock, a building, a flagpole, a sailboat at anchor—and then finds the
line with a grapnel.

Some crabbers stake territory they feel to be reliable
year after year. Gabrielson forages; that means following
the crabs around the river in their wanderings after
warmer water and food and in response to the arrival of
spring tides and the movement of the salt front. He sells
his crabs—what John calls "big, pretty, blue-clawed Hudson River crabs, the females with that touch of bright red
at the tips of their claws like nail polish"—to people who

meet his boat when it returns to the dock. What he doesn't sell then, he sells later from his house.

JOHN AGAIN: "The spring I worked with Gabrielson, I ate what came up in the nets. It was a very dry season; the salt advanced far up the river, and what I had mostly was saltwater fish. Flounder, mainly, and blackfish. I learned how to run a boat, how to get fish out of the net without ruining the net, and how to get fish out of the net without ruining the fish; shad are a very delicate fish, and you can easily destroy them if you're clumsy. I learned about calling the change of the tide by watching the river, so that you know when to pull the nets, and I began learning to pay attention to the shape of the bottom of the river, particularly the fasts—that is, the snags. Working with Bob, you begin to develop a picture of what the river is like under its surface—at least, the way you think it is—and the way it changes at different times of the year, for whatever reasons. Fasts arriving. You pull the net, and if it's cut or tangled from rocks you have one piece of information, or if the weights have mud on them then you immediately have an image of the color and consistency of the bottom. You of course already have a picture of what's swimming around on the bottom, from what's in the net.

"I began paying attention to all the changes in the life of the river—the seasonal movement of fish from one part of the river to another, the rise and decline of their runs, their migrations and arrivals, and the appearance of their fry. Toward the end of crabbing season, there are little shrimp everywhere—all over your arms when you pull the traps, all over the boat. From being with Gabrielson, you also learn some sort of sea sense, or river sense.

You learn how to run the river when the water is confused by currents or wind. It's not rolling or showing whitecaps, it's simply moving at cross-purposes—it has no proper plan to it. You learn to judge distances on the water and to develop a kind of night vision. You also learn what a big place the Hudson is. Even in its narrowest parts, the river is a big place. The first time I fished on my own, I had a couple of miles' run downriver to my nets, and it was night, and I just jumped into the boat and went out and looked for them. It then dawned on me that what I was after was a half-inch line in a three-mile strip of river.

"When that shad season was over, I moved to Garrison Landing, where I took up with a fisherman named Dave White, who taught me to drift-net for sturgeon. You cross the river in a rowboat during the last couple of hours before the tide. One person rows, and one pays out net over the stern. We had twelve hundred feet of net. You try to drift in the deepest part of the river, because sturgeon like deep water. Off Garrison is almost all deep water. While you sit beside the net, it drifts downstream on the final hour and a half of the tide. At slack water, it stops, pauses, then reverses itself on the flood tide, and you begin hauling as it returns upriver. The man retrieving the net removes the fish as he does it, and a really good drift-net fisherman will have the net and the fish in the boat by the time he returns to where he launched it. There are floats on the net's top line, and it lies beneath enough water so that a big boat can pass above the net without harming it. We caught catfish now and then, and the occasional striped bass. The sturgeon we pickled in brine—enough salt to float an egg—and then we smoked it, using cherry for the fire. What didn't go to our friends we sold locally. The season for sturgeon ends in July, and when it was over I built some crab pots and crabbed the rest of the summer, off Garrison. The next season, I decided to have a shad-fishing business with a friend. We built a boat in my garage and put all our nets together ourselves and had a great time and lost our shirts.

"Then, one day, Bob Boyle called me up. He was bringing a group of scientists to the Hudson to study striped bass, and since I had a boat and nets he wanted to know if I would catch fish for them. They stayed several days and set up a lab at West Point, and I caught fish, and they studied them, and then, after they left, Bob and I began talking. The Fishermen's Association had just got twenty-five thousand dollars from the power-plant settlements. Bob thought it would be a great idea if the association had a boat of its own, and even better if someone could be on it to help catch fish and patrol the river. The next spring, they resurrected the riverkeeper project. They asked me to do it, because during these last ten years I had had experience as an activist, a lobbyist, a legislative aide, and I had had investigative experience, time on the water—I had even sat for my Coast Guard license. I knew how to set nets, and I had worked with commercial fishermen. In the Exxon case, I used a little bit of all these things."

JOHN: "What happened is, there used to be a piece of Hudson River lore about tankers occasionally visiting the river and taking water for use in the Caribbean. The word was that they would anchor near Hyde Park and draw from deep springs that welled up from the bottom. You would hear it mentioned now and then, and people were more pleased by it than anything else. They felt that the taking of river water for use somewhere else was an encouraging sign. It meant that our water must be getting cleaner: 'Isn't it nice that the Hudson is clean enough so that people would take water from it down to the Caribbean?' Once the riverkeeper project got under way, though, I began getting calls from people saying that there were an awful lot of tankers out there. 'Every time I turn around, there's a tanker,' they'd say. One of the first callers was a state trooper, who told me he had heard that they weren't just anchoring, they were cleaning out their tanks. So we decided to watch tankers for a while. I had by now been on the water about a month.

"We began noting the tankers' arrivals. We had spies in New York City and Yonkers and Tarrytown and Hyde Park and Port Ewen, and every time a tanker passed New York Harbor I knew it, and I knew of its progress up the river. The first time I went out to look at one, in July of 1983, I had with me Andra Sramek, one of the people who work for the Fishermen's Association. Accompanying us was an NBC camera crew that was taping something about the riverkeeper project. We drove right up to the tanker, which was the Esso Palm Beach, moored off Hyde Park, and I raised the captain on the radio. 'Esso Palm Beach,' I said. 'This is the Riverkeeper. What are you discharging into the river?' He said, 'Fourteen thousand tons of seawater.' Now, hold the phone. From our point of view, this is already not right. This man is seventy-five miles up the river, discharging salt water in the freshwater part of the estuary, and the whole basis of the estuary is that the salt reaches only so far. So I asked him who he had permission from to discharge salt water into the Hudson River. 'With the permission of Exxon International,' he said. So I asked him if he planned on replacing that salt water with fresh water, and there was silence for what seems to me now, when I think about it, like several seconds, and then he came back on the radio and said, 'If you have any more questions, call Exxon International. They have many answers for many questions.' End of transmission. We had the NBC crew film the boat and the discharge, and we left.

"Around this time, I called up Exxon in New Jersey to inquire about these secret springs; I knew that someone there would find the idea of them amusing. I said that I was a historian doing research on the uses of Hudson River water, and I was looking for some information about the secret springs at Hyde Park, so they passed me from one public-information officer to another till I got one who was familiar with the story. I said I had heard that for decades tankers had been drawing pure water from springs at the bottom of the river and transporting it to the Caribbean. The guy had a big laugh over it—we both laughed—and he said, 'No, no, no, the reason they moor there is that it's a good anchorage, out of the channel.' I said, 'Oh, it's just an anchorage. I thought they were taking water,' and he said, 'Oh, I didn't say they weren't taking water. I just said there weren't these springs. They're drawing water, all right. And they're taking it to the Caribbean.'

" 'Oh, yeah?'

" 'Yeah, Aruba.'

" 'Oh, yeah?'

" 'Very dry island. Basically, we use the water for our refinery, but the island also uses it.'

"I said 'More so now than before?' and he said 'Who are you?' and I said 'I'm a Hudson River buff, doing some research.' I said 'Aren't there places closer to Aruba than the Hudson?' and he said 'We used to get water from the Río Orinoco, in Venezuela, but there were economic and political problems—they wanted to charge money for it.'

He said there was no place else on the East Coast where there was good navigation, fresh water, plus an anchorage. I think it was when I asked him how long this had been going on that he fell silent. He said, 'I think you want to know more than you are asking about.'

"At this point, we didn't really know anything about the scope of the operation—how many ships there were, and how often they were using the river. The next thing we discovered was that there could be more than one Exxon tanker on the river at one time. This was by accident. It was a day when a video crew was taping a documentary on the Hudson and wanted a shot of our boat racing across the river and another of it hauling a trawl. They planned to meet us at Hyde Park, in their own boat. Andra and I drove over to the Dutchess Community College field station and picked up some sample jars, and while we were on our way back we heard from the video crew. We told them there was a tanker on the river at Hyde Park and we wanted to get some samples from its discharges and if they wanted to meet us at it they could. They said fine. While we waited in the Riverkeeper, Andra and I discussed the best way to collect a sample. It's not easy. These are five-hundred-and-fifty-, six-hundred-foot tankers, big as whole towns. Some of the discharges come off the deck, high above the water, and some come from the hull, about twelve feet up. The discharges are like waterfalls. We wanted the video crew to film the tanker and the discharges. While we were studying the situation, the crew came on the radio and said, 'We're at the tanker, where are you?' We told them we were there, too, and said we would meet them at the bow, but when we got to the bow there was no one around. It took a little figuring and circling of the ship, but we realized we were at separate tankers. They were at a tanker several miles north, at Port Ewen. One was the Esso Shimizu, and one was the Esso Hong Kong. We got samples from both and packed them in ice, because these are volatile substances and keeping them cool keeps them less active and prevents their evaporating—plus if there are bacteria present it helps preserve an accurate count. The samples really stank. Very definite petrochemical smell—you could run your car on it. We later learned that these tankers had been carrying jet fuel. The analysis showed that the worst of the samples contained benzene, ethylbenzene, and toluene. There were eight hundred and fifty-five parts per billion of toluene in that one. Studies show that a hundred parts per billion will affect spawning in female striped bass. The tanker at Port Ewen couldn't have been more than fifteen hundred feet from the intake valve of the Port Ewen drinking-water supply.

"After that, I would follow tankers. I became obsessed. I would put up in the shallows between them in the dark and listen to the conversations of their captains on the radio. Once, I heard the one upriver warn the other that he was about to flush his tanks, so that the one downstream would know not to withdraw what the other had discharged. I heard a lot of their talk back and forth, but I never heard any of them say they were going to call Port Ewen and warn them.

"I began now doing legal research. I went to Albany and sat in an office where they had a set of McKinney's Consolidated Laws of New York, and then I went to the Natural Resources Defense Council, in Manhattan, and started checking federal laws and the navigation laws and the Clean Water Act and the Safe Drinking Water Act to see what might apply. It was apparent that there was no way those tankers could do what they were doing without permission, so I went to see if permission had been given.

It hadn't. I also began looking into the water trade—the buying and selling of water—with special emphasis on the Caribbean. I discovered that in addition to being a very arid island Aruba has no dependable water supply of its own. It has a desalinization plant, but I think it was broken. I learned that most of the Hudson water was going to the Lago Refinery but some was being diverted to the island's domestic water supply. We didn't begrudge them the water, really—just the way in which it was being taken.

"The reading and the phone calling lasted two months, just following leads from one thing to another. I got so I went to bed at night and couldn't wait to get up in the morning and learn more about the Caribbean water trade—what islands need water, why they need it, how they use it, and where they get it. At the United Nations I found a man who was an expert on water prices. In Barbados I discovered a man who was useful because people had come to him wanting to know where they could sell Hudson River water. In Norway, there was a man at the International Association of Independent Tanker Owners who had information: many tankers were idle at that time, and an idea for what to do with them was to have them carry water. In a *Christian Science Monitor* from 1947 I found an article that discussed the Lago Refinery and its dependence on water from the Hudson. We discovered that every once in a while the need for water in Aruba was so great that tankers would leave there empty for Hudson River water. I called the Aruba water works and asked if they were getting water from the Hudson, and they said yes. I asked if they were paying for it, and the man I spoke to said yes, and his attitude was 'You don't think water's free, do you?' All this was done before the case ever became public. When it came time to make the settlement, there was nothing Exxon could say that I didn't already know.

"By the time we had pieced together the story, we knew that what would happen with these tankers was this: Somewhere in the Northeast, they would unload their cargo of jet fuel or gasoline from the Lago Refinery. Then they'd return to the ocean to rinse out their tanks. There they would take on saltwater ballast, and then they'd go up the Hudson to Hyde Park. If there was already a tanker at Hyde Park, the second would continue to Port Ewen. If a third tanker arrived, there was room at Hyde Park for it to anchor. On at least one occasion, there were three tankers at Hyde Park. Once moored, the tankers would flush their salt water into the river. Then they would take aboard river water and rinse out the cargo tanks and the ballast tanks and discharge once again, then fill up with Hudson water. The process would take about thirty-six hours. When the boat was empty on one side and full on the other, it would list so hard that it would look grounded. It would look as if it were up on a shelf.

"During this time, I had lots of information about the activities of the tankers from people who live along the river. I got a letter in the mail—a greeting card, actually—from a man named Frank Parslow, in Port Ewen. He is a fisherman and lives on a steep slope several hundred feet above the river, and he has rigged a kind of small railroad—a tramway—to haul his fish up the slope from his dock. It's really a remarkable thing, and I know, because he told me, that it took three months to build—to find the right materials so that he didn't pay top dollar, and lying in bed at night trying to figure out how to do it. It chug-chug-chugs up the slope, and he meets it at the top and unloads it and smokes his fish in a small smokehouse. It looks like a wooden outhouse, and it has stainless-steel shelves, and he lines it with aluminum foil, and he makes about the best smoked shad on the river. All of it is spoken for immediately. He had kept track of the arrivals and departures and apparent business of many of these tankers over a period of time, and he sent it along, and when we were sitting down with the Exxon people I asked them 'How many tankers went up to Port Ewen and how many to Hyde Park over such-and-such a period?' and they said 'Well, we don't really keep track of that kind of thing, but not many,' and I was able to pull out Frank Parslow's greeting card and talk turkey. From here and there we were able to learn that over two years a hundred and seventy-seven tanker trips had been made up the river, at who knows what cost to the estuary.

"We notified Exxon of our intent to sue under the federal Clean Water Act. Sent a letter to the chairman of the board. Looked up the address in the phone book. When we finally went public, the reaction was mainly outrage. The facts were that the largest corporation in the world was bringing its tankers up the river and flushing their holds and stealing water. The water thievery was what got attention, but what bothered me most was that they were rinsing out their holds. As far as I was concerned, the thievery was just icing on the cake, but I was willing to stress whatever issue motivated people.

"Exxon's reaction, essentially, was denial. Getting them to talk was a slow process. There was a lot of posturing on both sides. Early in our negotiations toward a settlement, Exxon told us that they were perfectly willing to wage a campaign to win public sympathy, and I told them, 'Wait a minute. You're an oil company. You *can't* win public sympathy. Who's going to believe you?' We met before Christmas and signed agreements around Easter. We settled out of court for half a million dollars and the commitment to discontinue the practice until the state legislature addressed the issue of tanker discharges, which they decided to regulate in 1985. Of that figure, the Fishermen's Association got half. The rest went to the Open Space Institute, an environmental organization. The state then settled separately for a million and a half. As much as I would like to say it was our tough negotiating style that made them give in, I think what made them give in is that the story would not go away. We made a great effort to keep it in the papers. We sent out information as it seemed necessary. Piece by piece. We knew the whole story to begin with, but if we had given it all out at once it might have died. Really, we battered at them in the press, but why we did is we were trying to send a message: We are watching the Hudson; we are keeping our eyes on the river. It wasn't the first time anyone had said it, but it's always important that it be heard, because the river, for all its apparent immensity, is fragile.

"What I think of as an example is Diamond Reef. It's off New Hamburg, by Wappinger's Creek, below Poughkeepsie. It's in the middle of the river, and it's about a hundred yards long, and at low tide it's perhaps five feet under the surface. It's very well marked on the charts. A person consulting the charts couldn't miss it; it says 'Diamond Reef,' with the added information that it's rocky, and the depth noted. There's also a light there. But we get these cowboys from the South running barges up the river. They've brought these things up here and are trying to reach a tank farm in Poughkeepsie, and they're tugboat operators who may have been on the Hudson once in their lives, if at all—it's anybody's guess—or they don't have the proper charts, or they think they can save some time by squeezing between the buoys, which means leaving the channel, and they run the river like a racetrack and plow

right into the reef and break up the barges and spill gasoline and oil and coal and gravel on it and shave a few
feet off the reef every time. The tankers that come up the
river are plenty larger than the tugboats and the barges,
and they don't come near the reef—don't even scratch it.

"It's very rich in fish life, Diamond Reef. A lot of food
for fish congregates there, and to have barges running up
on it and dumping gasoline and heating oil and coal
doesn't help. It also makes the Army Corps of Engineers
want to blow up Diamond Reef. What they would destroy I'm not exactly sure, but if you go out and drift
over it at the right time of year you catch many striped
bass. It's not hit or miss. It's constant year after year. They
are there one moment or they are not, but over time
they are there. All along the river are people who from
patience and through observation know the quarter of a
mile where they live with great accuracy and detail—the
comings and goings of fish and wildlife, and the seasons,
and the changes along the riverbank. There is probably
someone like that for every quarter-mile of river. It's not
because of a textbook or a pamphlet or the work of some
researcher that we know about the life of Diamond Reef;
we know about it because of a man who fishes it obses-
sively and keeps records.

"With estuaries, there is the idea of microhabitats.
Which is to say that with a place like the Hudson, over a
certain period of time—say, a week, or several days—there
could be an area the size of a football field, or maybe a
city block, that just for that moment could be the most
important part of the river, because it's a place where fish
gather, or spawning takes place. A place where certain fish
and other life forms congregate, perhaps because of food
or protection or some reason we don't know about yet.
The Hudson is still largely unresearched. Unstudied. We

know, for example, that the Hudson is the home of the blue crab, but we don't know where they spawn; we may already have lost it. Out of a hundred and fifty-four miles of estuary, how many reefs, holes, bays, shallows, inlets, marshes, coves, and flats can there be like that? Where might they be at any one time? In what order do they shift around the river? Is there a sequence or is it chance? Do the same places remain important year after year? Do new ones replace them? What ones are more important than others? How many are active at one time? How many are threatened and need protection? How many have been destroyed and need to be restored? How do you revive them? As attractive as issues like the Exxon tankers can be, I get more pleasure from working on the small spots. A place here, a place there. An important part of being involved with the Hudson is the mystery of where those places are."

......................................

*The Uncommitted Crime*

ANGOON IS A SHACKY, TENACIOUS, REMOTE, and defiant little frontier-speck of an Indian town on Admiralty Island in southeast Alaska. It is surrounded by wilderness. Convocations of eagles turn and circle above it like figures in a mobile. When they land on the long, springy branches of a spruce or a hemlock or a cedar or a pine, the branches shake and all the other birds leave. You can walk up close then and stare at the eagles and they will stare back at you. The look in their eyes is kind of mad and impatient and half-witted. Their feet and beaks are the color of the yellow on the shaft of a pencil. From a distance their bodies blend with the body of the tree, so that all you can see of them is their white heads, like light bulbs. In the spring, when the herring are running, there are more bald eagles on Admiralty Island than in all forty-nine other states. Some of the eagles stay around all year. When the fishermen catch bullheads, or black bass, or rockfish, or some other fish they don't care to keep, they leave the fish floating for the eagles. Sometimes one launches himself and soars into the air until he is just a tiny, wheeling stick-figure cross against the sky, then returns and strikes a cat on the beach in front of the town.

Admiralty Island is ninety-six miles long and thirty miles wide at its widest part, it has seven hundred and twenty miles of coastline, and Angoon is the only town on it. Approximately six hundred and thirty people live there; according to the phone book, sixty-seven have phones. The largest part of them are Tlingit, which is properly pronounced "Thleen-git," but more commonly "Klink-Kit," and are stubborn enough in their resolve to preserve their ancestral ways that Angoon is often referred to as the last outpost of Tlingit culture. The town is built on a small spit of land. At its narrowest point there is room for four or five houses, built end to end and almost as close as the cars on a train. On one side of the spit, the west, are the long perspectives of water that are Chatham Strait, with the mountains of Baranof and Chichagof islands beyond. On the east is an inlet splitting into channels leading inland. The Tlingit knew their way around the channels, and knew the oddities of the tides, and had no fear of an attack from the water. Looking at the placement of Angoon on a map, one sometimes feels that it is as if the Indians who settled it had sought out the most isolated, backs-to-the-wall, they-can-only-come-at-us-from-one-end place to put up their town. North of Angoon is a small woods, perhaps half a mile of it, then water. The Tlingit, while brave to the point of fearlessness, were also obsessed spirit thinkers, and the idea that the woods were full of crafty, witching, and sinister forces made a lot of sense to them. Also, they didn't care much for bears. A reason one sometimes hears for why Angoon is where it is, is that bears could get at it from only one side.

The older section of town describes roughly the shape of an arc. It includes about thirty-five houses. Seen from the strait they rise in rows up the side of the hill like the rows on the keyboard of a typewriter. Until the middle of the nineteen-seventies, when money from the federal government made it possible to clear land and build houses on the hill above the old town, everyone in Angoon lived in one of the old houses. Most are of simple plank and frame construction and are weathered to soft colors or scuffed back to plain wood. Some are built gable end to the water, Tlingit-style, and some are sideways to it. Most have peaked roofs finished with tin, two windows downstairs in the front, with a door between them, and a window upstairs above the door. In the windows of many are children.

The majority of old houses have tribal affiliations. They were built late in the nineteenth century or early in this one and are smaller versions of the houses the Tlingit built in back times. The houses are known by names the Indians gave them to commemorate some aspect of their past or a characteristic of someone who lived in them. Some of the names are Iron Bark House, Springwater House, Killer Whale House, Killer Whale Chasing the Seal House, Killer Whale Tooth House, Log Jam House, Mountain Valley House, On Top of the Fort House, End of the Trail House, Middle of the Village House, Bear House, Raven House, and Raven Bones House.

On the front of the Killer Whale House, in the triangle made by the top of the door and under the notch of the roof, are painted two killer whales, in the Tlingit style.

Each is about ten feet long. Their heads face away from each other and their tails almost touch above the door. The fins on their backs rise to the top of the upstairs window. They are black and turquoise and red and all but precisely match figures painted on the housefront in the nineteenth century and later covered over; the present-day image was drawn from the outline of the original, which showed faintly through the paint. At one time there were several painted houses in town. All were painted over or had their images removed and taken indoors around 1929 to make Angoon presentable for a meeting of the Alaska Native Brotherhood, an organization created to oppose bad treatment of Indians by white people. Its members believed that the way into the new world was not through the past but by learning to speak English and live and behave like white men.

The houses in Angoon rarely come up for sale. Some are tribal property, others have titles that are in dispute. All require a cash sale. Because they have problems with titles and no foundations, it is not possible to mortgage them. Also it is costly to insure them, because they catch fire so easily.

THE climate of Admiralty is that of a subarctic rain forest. The woods are so thickly overgrown that it is very hard to walk in them, except where trails have been cleared; most people in Angoon have never been to the other side of the island. Around Angoon are a trail about three miles long leading south from the town, through bear territory, to a burying ground and a ferry terminal, and one running northwest about half a mile, not through bear territory, also to a burying ground and beyond it to an outcropping of land called Danger Point. The woods are so damp that it is difficult to start a fire in them. In the nineteenth century, Aleksandr Baranof, the Russian explorer and governor of all Russian activities in North America, tried to burn down the trees around Sitka, forty-five miles west of Angoon, because they gave protection to the Indians, and had to give up and cut them down instead, because he could not make them catch.

The wilderness is mainly hemlock and spruce, among which are concentrations of lodgepole pine, and two kinds of cedar—red and yellow. Here and there are a few lowland clearings, called muskegs, filled with grasses and sedges, and below them tidal lowgrounds called salt chucks. Along the sides and tops of some of the mountains are meadows. Crossing them and winding through the woods are bear trails, which do not look like the paths deer scuff into the forest floor, but are simply one paw print following another in line, the marks of generations of bears walking carefully through the forest in the footprints of their ancestors.

Hundreds of bears inhabit the wilderness. Admiralty has the highest density of bears in America, and it is possible that there may be a thousand or more of them in the forest. The bears are a type of grizzly. They can charge at forty miles an hour. Even at a distance you can often hear them for a long time before they come into view. I saw bears only once in Angoon, in a field beside the road, and my recollection is that they were the size of small mobile homes. The dogs in the town mostly keep them away, but if a bear has any real reason to come to town it will. Sometimes people wake in the morning and see them on the beach.

I went to Angoon for the first time in January, and then I went back in April. I rented a room in a lodge that serves hunters and fishermen over the summer. When I spoke to someone there on the phone from New York City and asked how I would find the place, he said it was right next to the airport. I flew from New York to Seattle to Juneau and then boarded a plane on which I was the only passenger. It loaded the mail and some packages and landed about half an hour later on the water of the inlet and coasted up to a dock. I stood a few minutes beside the wilderness with my suitcase, and then a man showed up to collect a package that had come over on the plane. I asked if he knew where the lodge was and he pointed to a path. On both of my trips I was the only customer. My room had a metal door with a bullet hole in it about eye-level, like a peephole in an apartment door, which some-one had tried to patch. The hole was made by a hunter who was cleaning his rifle and didn't remember it was loaded. Afterwards he was furious that no one had come to see if he had been hurt.

The lodge is about a mile from town along the road that leads to the ferry terminal, at Killisnoo, once an In-dian fort, then in the nineteenth century a white man's town that had a whale works and a herring-reduction plant that mainly went out of business around 1915. The town lingered through several fires, then burned almost completely and in the nineteen-twenties was abandoned. The road is about three miles long and is the only road in Angoon. It is closed on both sides by trees, except for a small stretch by the town highway barn, where one can look into the inlet. The tide there rising and falling and rushing through the rips makes a sound like traffic. From the road you can see some rocks on which cormorants stand. As the tide rises the cormorants edge closer and closer until all of them are bunched together like a bou-quet. The road is made from gravel and dirt. During pe-riods of dryness, each car is followed by a tail of dust.

People drive back and forth along the road for no particular reason except to get out of the house and move around, or be alone for a while, or court, or look at the water, or from nerves and restlessness, or just to feel like they are going somewhere. Mothers calming fretful babies sometimes put them in the car and drive them to Killisnoo. The best radio reception in town is along certain parts of the road, so when the high school basketball team is away at the state tournament, people get in their cars at night and drive out to the ferry terminal and park with their engines running and the heat on and listen to the game, or go down by the float where the plane arrives, or pull to the side of the road somewhere along the way. The reception pulses and fades and gets covered by other stations, so the people are constantly moving their cars, to find the strongest signal. At half time they get out and visit with each other, standing behind the cars under the huge Alaskan sky, their faces the color of a blush in the taillights. They call this "going up the road." The road is a little more than two cars wide and has several narrow curves. When the town finally had its first head-on collision, it turned out that the people in both cars were from the same family.

In the winter, smoke from the chimneys stays close to the ground and drifts like fog past the windows. The ceiling of the sky is never very far overhead. The tops of the mountains appear and disappear in the clouds. When the tops are covered, the mountains look like plateaus, or as if some kind of abrasion from the sky had sanded them flat. The sun is rarely visible. The sky is almost always white. When the road is full of snow and the crows are crossing the sky, it is like watching black-and-white television. Children ride their bicycles on the frozen road. Crows land on the tin roofs and do a clicky, skidding little dance to get a purchase. They make a hard, ratchety sound in the backs of their throats like castanets. Ravens twice the size of crows strut down the street, stepping aside for cars. The dogs sometimes run up to them and bark in their faces, and the ravens, as big as the dogs, don't even move. Beside the ravens, the crows look like discarded versions of the final design. People sometimes shoot the dogs, for no apparent reason. Not long ago a family let their dog out and someone shot it, and they bought another and someone shot this one as it sat on their porch.

There is no bank, and no restaurant or bar or cafe; Angoon is dry. People buy liquor in Sitka or Juneau and bring it over in the trunks of their cars on the ferry. The street through the old part of town is one way, but no one knows which way, because a vote has never been taken to decide. On the side of a hill in the center of town are five totem poles.

The beach is a fine, powdery sand that is the color of old copper. Dogs and ravens and gulls and crows leave their prints along the line of the tide. People leave bicycles and old tires and car parts and deer hides and rubber gloves and shoes one at a time and bent-up rusted mysterious-looking pieces of metal that you can almost but not quite divine the purpose of. The Tlingit at Angoon used to throw their trash on the beach and let the tide take it out, which has not made them popular with archaeologists. Every now and then the tide uncovers one of the old blue-glass beads that the Russians used in trade with the Tlingit.

The people I passed on the unpaved streets or in the aisles of the town's only store were neither friendly nor unfriendly. Some were curious at seeing an outsider, some acted as if I were invisible, some responded when I nod-ded or waved as they passed in their cars. More than one person, I noticed, wore a T-shirt that had on it the name of the town and a phonetic inscription in a language I did not recognize. Beneath the inscription was the date "October 26, 1882." The first person I asked would not tell me what it said, and the second wouldn't either. The third studied me, then looked away, then looked back and said that what it meant was, "The day we suffered for the crime we did not commit."

THE name "Tlingit" denotes a language, not a tribe. Historically, fourteen tribes throughout southeast Alaska spoke Tlingit. The one that settled Angoon was called the Hootsnoowoos, which means "great den of bears" and was spelled a number of ways, including Hoochinoos and Kootznahoos and Hootznahoos. The Tlingit occupied the coastline and riverbanks and to some extent the forest along an approximately five-hundred-mile strip of land running from Yakutat Bay in the north to just below the Canadian border. There was no alliance among the tribes and no occasion on which all fourteen ever acted together. All considered their society to be divided between two lineages, designated raven and eagle. The lineages—what anthropologists call moieties—are divided into clans. In any Tlingit village are members of a number of clans, but no clan is represented in all. In Angoon today, on the raven side, are beaver, sockeye, dog salmon, and raven, as well as, by marriage, tern, frog, humpback, and coho. On the eagle side are killer whale, eagle, shark, bear, wolf, and, by marriage, thunderbird. It is common to place the name of the lineage ahead of the clan, as in raven beaver, or to precede the name of the clan with the name of the town that it comes from, as in Angoon raven, or Kake killer whale.

In past times, clans controlled grounds for hunting and fishing and owned houses. In addition, they possessed artifacts such as hats and masks and robes and dishes and totems and carvings and bowls, as well as the rights to various legends, dances, and ceremonies pertaining to their background. The Tlingit practice was to fish and hunt the grounds belonging to one's lineage. To enter the territory of the other required permission. When the white men arrived, they fished and hunted anywhere they wanted to. The canneries sent their fleets wherever they thought there were fish. The Tlingit had trouble understanding how a civilization supposedly superior to their own could be less honorable.

A village had no formal organization. No clan held rights above any other, except what their wealth and power allowed them to claim, and there were no chiefs, only heads of clan houses. The opposite lineage was responsible to the other for burying its dead. In return, the indebted clan threw a feast, called a potlatch, which long ago involved dances and rituals and speeches and gifts, and became something more edgy and intense after whiskey and white men's trading goods became part of it. A Tlingit was allowed to marry only a person from the opposite lineage. Clans today are debased from their former authority, but nearly all Tlingit observe this prohibition. In Angoon, kids sometimes complain that all the attractive prospects belong to their lineage.

Among the clans the significant line of descent was not the father's, but the mother's. A child became a member of his or her mother's clan. The most important man in the life of a boy was his mother's brother, to whom he was apprenticed and whose legacy he inherited. A boy called his ancestral home "the land of my uncles."

.  .  .

N O T much is known about Angoon before the twentieth century because not many white people had been there. Also, most of the time when they were, the town was drunk. One man who stopped there in the nineteenth century wrote that he witnessed "a drunken revel of indescribable abandon, during which naked and half-naked men and women dragged themselves about the place." A missionary travelling wrote, "Tuesday we reached Angoon, the chief town of the Hootznahoos. It is beautifully situated and has a population of four hundred and ten. But we did not remain long as the whole town was drunk." John Muir, the naturalist, visited Angoon. He wrote that from half a mile away he could hear men and women screaming and yelling and bellowing and grunting and groaning. He described the houses of the town as a "chain of alcoholic volcanoes," and he said that it was the first time in his life he had understood the term "howling drunk." People describing the effects of alcohol on the Indians of Alaska often used the term "whiskey howl." A whole town drunk was a "whiskey storm."

The word "hooch" as a term for liquor is derived from a corruption of "Hoochinoo." The Hootsnoowoos were taught to make rum by an American soldier named Brown, who married a woman from Angoon and moved there around 1879. It had been introduced to the Tlingit by Russian convicts around 1796; fur traders liked to use it as trade bait because they noticed they could come to better terms with a drunk Indian. Once the Hootsnoowoos learned to make it, they spurned liquor in trade; what the white man offered was not strong enough. The ingredients of hoochinoo were sugar, molasses, flour, yeast, and anything else fermentable, mainly rice, potatoes, and raisins. They would carry gallons of it in their canoes to Sitka and sell it under the name Hootznoo. The regulations preventing white men from giving liquor to the Indians were put in place before the Indians learned how to make it. Nothing prevented an Indian from walking into a store and buying the ingredients or making it himself.

Hooch was colorless and smelled bad, and from impatience the Indians often drank it hot from the still. Trading posts had houses for the Indians to stay in while they did their business. The Hootsnoowoos often got in trouble for bringing liquor to trade, or for moving in to the houses and setting up stills and kicking off a drunk. The white people were afraid of drunk Indians, but continued to sell them molasses. They also continued to ban selling them liquor and to profit from offering alternatives. One was a patent medicine called Painkiller, which was a-hundred-and-two proof and about two percent opium. Painkiller was especially popular in Killisnoo. Empty bottles of it could be found all over its streets, and a gaunt old man there who was addicted to it spent nearly all his time in a stupor and was known as Painkiller. Whenever he was without it, he was said to be dying. Indians desperate to be drunk would also drink bay rum and sometimes perfume. Before the white man, Indians only drank water.

WHEN a Tlingit was about to die he would sometimes say, "This house is beginning to fill with spirits. They are waiting for me." The Tlingit believed that touching a corpse was dangerous, so when they felt that a sick person was drawing near death they would bathe him and dress him in his best clothes. A corpse was removed from a house by means of a door cut usually into the side of the house and sometimes into the back, or through a hole made in the side by removing a plank. A body could never be taken through the front door because it was felt that the dread mystery of death would then be on the threshold. After the body, a dead dog was thrown through the opening, then some sand or some ashes. The door was sealed or the plank put back in place to keep the spirit of death from finding its way in. The purpose of the sand was to make a path for the soul on his way to the land of the dead. The purpose of the ashes I wish I knew. The dog had several purposes, each apparently local. In some places it was thought that the dog confused the ghost believed to be waiting outside to carry the soul to the land of the dead and kept him from harming anyone living; in others, that the spirit of death would inhabit the dog and not be able to return to the house and that if no dog were taken, someone else would be. In others, the dog was meant to protect the dead man travelling along the trail to the afterlife. In others, it was thought that the spirit of death had come to inhabit the dog and it must therefore be thrown out of the house, and in others, that it would take with it all traces of the disease.

The bodies of the dead were covered with blankets and burned on pyres of cedar or spruce. Sometimes when a murderer had been slain by the family of the victim, the two bodies would be burned under the same blanket. Cremation was essential to the Tlingit. One of the ways that they imagined the afterlife was as a place warmed by a fire. Those who had been cremated were able to stand close to the fire, and those who had not, who had drowned, for example, and whose bodies had not been recovered, had to stand behind the others and were always cold. This belief made it difficult for the Tlingit to accept the idea of Christian burial. Satisfaction was what early missionaries to Alaska saw on the faces of the people they lectured on the subject of the fires of hell. Not until they began to describe hell as cold and forbidding did they get the response they hoped for.

The Tlingit conceived of three levels to the afterlife. Warriors killed in battle and people killed by accident went to a place in the sky called "above people's country," where they lived with plenty of warmth and light and food, especially grease. For servants they had the souls of the warriors they had killed as well as those of the slaves sacrificed for their benefit at their mortuary feasts. Because of the expectation of this reward, Tlingit had no fear in battle. The Tlingit thought of the sky as being solid, and in the shape of a dome. The horizon they thought of as something like the eaves of a house, and this is where those who died a natural death would go. This place was called "sky eaves land." When the spirit was released by the fire from its body, it would begin a trip along a narrow, rocky, overgrown, bush-tangled trail. If his relatives cried too much at his funeral, then the ground he crossed was swampy. Bye and bye the trail widened and came to an end at the shore of a green water, across which the spirit could see human shapes the size of mosquitoes. He would call them but they didn't answer. After a while he would fall asleep, then wake to see a canoe coming toward him. The canoe carried him across the water, where he joined his relations who had died before him. Those who had been cremated stood by the fire, and the rest stood some distance off, shivering. The souls in the lowest level of the afterlife inhabited a place called the village of the dead and suffered hunger and cold. Russian Orthodox missionaries tried to get the Tlingit to organize their sense of the afterlife into a hierarchy and to call the person in charge of the lowest level the Chief of the Below, but the idea never really took. The Tlingit called the souls of this level "the bones people."

Death by drowning was what the Tlingit feared most. The body of a person who drowned was believed to be claimed by land otter men and turned into one of their own. First the drowned man would grow fur, then his speech would become confused, then he would start walking on his elbows and knees, and then he would grow a tail. On seeing anyone he knew in the forest he would try to be recognized in order to be cremated and have his spirit set free to join his ancestors by the fire. The souls of drowned people whose bodies sank sat in deep mud beneath a ledge over which flowed a cascade which kept them trapped. Children who drowned were thought to be imprisoned somewhere in the earth. The souls of very bad people went to an immense open space between the winds, where they never had any rest.

Eventually the Tlingit began to assume some ideas of the Christian afterlife. The Tlingit term for their version of hell was "dog heaven." It was located between the earth and the place in the sky where the northern lights appear. It was where the dog spirits went, as well as suicides and murderers and witches.

For the funeral the Tlingit would engage professional mourners, women who would paint their faces black and sit beside the body and cry. A mourner's first tear would run straight down her cheek, making a track. Then she would turn her head at an angle, so that the next tear also made a track. Mourners were paid by the number of tracks they could show.

It was Tlingit custom to burn on his pyre certain of a man's possessions that he might find useful in the afterlife.

For a while after they had first accepted Christianity they continued to do this, except that instead of burning the goods they left them sitting on top of the grave. One man put a mattress on a man's grave, another a sewing machine, and another a record player, and they all stayed there until they had absorbed all the weather they could and then fell apart.

THE Tlingit believed that epidemics were caused by spirits who arrived in sailing ships or steamboats or sailboats or canoes. The boats were called the boats of sickness, and only shamans could see them. As people died they got into the boats, and when the epidemic had run its course the boats left. Like the Indians of the plains, the Tlingit were subject to diseases that were brought to them by Europeans and for which they had no natural defenses. Tuberculosis was sometimes called the white man's disease or the Great White Plague. Scarlet fever, smallpox, measles, and syphilis came from the Russians. Spaniards travelling north from Mexico in 1775 also brought smallpox, and American fur traders and workers for the American Telegraphic Expedition in 1866 also brought syphilis. In addition, there were epidemics of typhoid in 1819, 1848, and 1855. An epidemic of smallpox in 1836 killed half the Tlingit. Many of its survivors lost faith in their shamans, who could do nothing against the disease, and turned to the doctors at Sitka instead, and that changed something forever. Yakutat, the Tlingit village farthest to the north, escaped that epidemic, and for that their shaman took credit.

Shamans were not cremated, because it was believed that their bodies would not burn. The first night of his death a shaman was left lying in the corner of the house closest to where he was when he died. Each night of the next three he was moved to another corner, and on the fifth day he was taken to his grave. Usually a shaman was buried sitting, and facing the water, on a headland, or in a cave, or on a cliff. Indians passing would throw some tobacco, or fish oil, or some dried salmon into the water, saying as they did so something like, "Let me have luck," or, "Don't let me die," or, "Don't let the wind blow too strongly on my boat." Anyone who came close enough to the shore would leave his offering there. The Tlingit believed that a person could pick up a sickness by getting too close to a shaman's grave, or by handling anything that had belonged to a dead shaman. American tourists often raided shamans' graves and took with them whatever they wanted, and the Indians couldn't believe that they didn't fall down and die.

Not all shamans had the same powers, but most were believed able to invoke spirits who could help them make predictions, or protect warriors, or influence the fortunes of a hunt or a fishing trip, or change the weather. One was famous for having survived a drowning. A war party usually took a shaman with it. The shaman would lie under a robe in the bottom of the canoe and go into a trance to report where the enemy was and how many there were. Some shamans were able to hold burning objects in their hands and not be harmed, and to put them in their mouths and take them out and all that would happen is their tongues would smoke. Some could bring the dead back to life. All were believed to have the ability to predict their own deaths, to discover witches and undo their spells, and to call up demons to attack anyone who opposed them, which made other Indians scared of them.

In appearance, the main differences between a shaman and any other Tlingit were that the shaman never washed, and never cut his hair. To keep the hair out of his face he used spruce sap, which made the hair hard and stiff and caused it when he moved to make a sound like wooden balls hitting each other.

Most of the time when a Tlingit fell sick he believed that the sickness was the result of a spell thrown by a witch. The Tlingit believed that witches, for convenience, could become animals, especially cranes, porpoises, sea lions, and owls. A dog barking toward the graveyard was believed to be warning that a witch was about. The Tlingit also believed witches could fly. Their favorite place to fly to, after the arrival of the missionaries, was the cemetery, where they would dig up graves and use certain remains for witchcraft. The most common way of bewitching a person was taking some of his fingernails or hair or a piece of his clothing or some saliva and placing it inside the corpse of a person or a dog; as the corpse rotted, so would the victim. By means of spells cast over a person's hair, a witch could also cause him to go blind; by hexing his fingernails he could cause a person's hand to become paralyzed; and by witching his saliva he could cause him to spit himself to death. Slow, wasting diseases, like tuberculosis, natural to the damp territory, helped suggest witchcraft. In Angoon, in 1957, a sixteen-year-old girl claimed that her baby had been killed by a witch. She and a girl who was twelve held séances during which they made predictions, one of which involved naming people who would fall sick. Anyone who didn't take them seriously they called a nonbeliever, a category that included most people, until a viral epidemic arrived. On one occasion then, the older girl told a man that something would happen that night to convince him that she and her friend were telling the truth, and the next day the man said that the night before he had seen a man turn into a bird and fly away.

When a person wanted to employ a shaman, he would make a pile of robes and furs and food on his floor and send for the shaman. If the reason for the summons of the shaman was a suspicion of witchcraft, the messenger would stand outside the shaman's door and give a particular call, in some towns a phrase that would translate, "A Tlingit is sick." The shaman would pretend not to understand, and the call would be repeated three times. It was thought that somewhere inside the messenger's voice the shaman could hear the voice of the witch, and that this was the reason for repeating the call. The shaman would then go and look at the goods and go home and send word whether he would accept the case. Always he was paid in advance. If he was not able to come through with a cure, he would claim that rival spirits had interfered with his work and he would have to perform another ceremony, for which he would again have to be paid.

White people really hated shamans. They felt they were cynical and thievish and conniving and predatory and corrupt. Of course they may have been, but it is also easy to find in those attitudes the frustration of the missionary and his contempt for a culture he is bent on destroying. In any case, what the white people hated most was the persecution of witches. To cure illness, the shaman would name a witch. The white people said that the shaman would always name some old woman with no family, or a child of a family with no standing, or a person against whom he had a grudge. To prove he was correct in his choice a shaman would fill his hat with water and ask three people to come and look into it and see the face of the witch. Either they were accomplices, or afraid of him, because it rarely happened that the shaman was contradicted.

If the witch happened to be a powerful person, he was

asked to lower the sickness to the bottom of the sea. Lowering meant taking the thing responsible for the illness and dropping it into the water. If the witch had no one to defend him, he was tied up and tortured or beaten or stoned, and then left to die from hunger or thirst, or on the beach to drown, or was buried alive in a box.

Before the arrival of the Europeans and the Americans, shamans used to live in the towns among the people, but missionaries and the men in charge of what civil law there was made the shamans' lives more difficult, so they began to move into the woods. One of the naval commanders in Sitka at the end of the last century liked to hunt shamans. The ones he was disciplining, usually for having tortured witches, he subjected to the humiliation of being bathed and having their hair cut and then made to promise in front of other Tlingits never to practice again. Before doing this, he offered the shaman the opportunity to use all his powers to bring down any plagues he cared to against him and his crew. The commander's name was Henry Glass, and what he liked to do for sport was to have a shaman captured and brought aboard his boat. Glass would receive the shaman as an equal and after a certain amount of talk in front of other Tlingits about the shaman's life and his powers and charms Glass would announce that he was also a shaman and had special powers, and he would suggest that the two of them compete. Glass would then have a battery brought on deck and would ask the shaman to hold in his hands the wires attached to its poles. The force of the shock would cause the shaman to scream and his body to convulse, and after that, shaving his head and extracting the promise to retire were pretty much formalities, but Glass did them anyway.

The last full-blooded Tlingit shaman was a woman who practiced at least until 1934, in Angoon.

. . .

## III

THE person I spent the most time with in Angoon is Matthew Kookesh. The surnames of most Tlingit are simple,
English-sounding first names such as Fred, Jack, Jim, Nel-
son, and Frank. Some were given to their ancestors by
missionaries, some by timekeepers at the canneries who
were unable to spell the more complicated Tlingit names,
and some are the result of a shortening of a nickname
given by a white person, such as White Water Jack. Matthew's is one of the few unreconstructed Tlingit surnames
in town. The reason for this, he believes, is that Tlingit
names beginning with K—Kanosh, Kitka, and Klushkan
are others—were easy enough for white people to pro-
nounce and so were left alone. Matthew is only half Tlingit. His mother is Mexican. She and his father met when
he was sent to an Indian hospital in New Mexico to recover from pleurisy. He had signed on to join an expedition to the South Pole and was getting his physical when
the pleurisy was diagnosed. They lived in Mexico for a
while, then came back to Angoon in the thirties, then left
and came back two more times. His mother was adopted
by the bear clan. His father is dead, but his mother lives
in town. She tells Matthew that he spoke Spanish as a
child, but he doesn't remember it. Matthew is small and
slightly bowlegged, Tlingit-style, but he is solidly built.
His hair is black but not as straight as pure-blood Tlingit
and also is beginning to recede. He has a high forehead, a
long nose and dark eyes, and a heavy beard which he
shaves infrequently, and which gives him a piratical look.
He lives with his wife, Jackie, who is Tlingit and grew up
in Juneau, and their children Nadja and Matthew, who are
teenagers, and Nikolai, who is two.

Matthew is a bear and Jackie is a coho. Matthew's Tlingit name is Yaanustuk. He was told by an uncle that his Indian name has to do with thunder and lightning and comes from the Thunderbird house, but that was all he was told and he wishes he knew more. Kookesh describes an action made by the finning tails of salmon over their nests.

Matthew has four brothers and four sisters. One sister is in Sitka, and one is in Seattle; the rest of his brothers and sisters live in Angoon. He has no uncles in town, and that is difficult for him, because Tlingit society is still enough intact that a man without an uncle is detached from his culture. Matthew is keenly interested in knowing the myths and legends and ceremonies of the past and feels his separation from them as a deprivation. Tlingit is not a written language, so Tlingit culture is a memory culture. When cultures of this kind intersect white cultures, children raised in memory cultures learn about their past from their grandparents, who mind them while the parents are working. Once grown, the children go out into the white world to make a living and often are disappointed and return to the elders wanting to know more about how they lived. In Angoon the younger people in this position feel that the elders are sometimes possessive about what they know, because the air of secrecy gives them power. Also there is the difficulty that no one under forty in Angoon speaks Tlingit, although some can understand it. For conversations of any significance, the elders use their own language. Sometimes, in referring to the past, they use the phrase "the canoe days."

Matthew and Jackie live in the old part of the town, in a house that they bought for fifteen thousand dollars and have all but rebuilt. The walls downstairs are wainscoting taken from the superintendent's house at the old cannery out at Hood Bay ten miles from Angoon. For years people had tried to remove it, with no luck, and then Jackie figured out that, because of the tongue-and-groove construction, it had to be taken off the wall a board at a time from the top, not the bottom. Two picture windows at the front of the house frame the inlet. Ducks spin down the tide rips like bath toys. The sun rises in front of the house and sets behind it. Ten thousand dollars for the down payment came from selling the trailer they were living in over in Sitka while they attended Sheldon Jackson Junior College, and the rest of the money Matt made on the pipeline and from fishing. The house is not a clan house, but now that it is in such fine shape people have tried to claim that it is, in hopes of getting it out of Matt and Jackie's hands, or getting some money for it.

October to May, Matthew works for the Alaska Department of Fish and Game, in the subsistence division. In Alaska "subsistence" is the word used to describe the practice of hunting and fishing for one's food. He has an office in a building in the shape of a cross and standing on top of the hill in the center of town. His office is down a long, dark hallway; the secretary in one of the other offices on the corridor turns the light off, because it shines in her eyes. A small plaque over his door says "Subsistence." His name, among others, is on four technical papers the department has published—one about crabs, one about salmon fishing in the Chilkat and Chilkoot River drainages on the mainland, one about salmon fishing in the salt lake in the interior of the island, and one about logging and how it has affected wildlife in southeast Alaska. The rest of the year Matthew fishes commercially for halibut and king salmon, and hunts. He also guides sport fishermen. In the winter he walks the beaches on a minus tide, turning over rocks and peering into crevices for octopus—what the Tlingit called devilfish—to use as bait for halibut when the season arrives.

Matthew was born in Juneau in 1950. In those days Angoon had no high school, so children were required to attend the one in Wrangell, where they would board for the year and come home only in the summer. After high school he went into the Navy and was stationed in Hawaii. Around 1968 his father began the oil station in town—that is, the business that supplied heating oil and gasoline to Angoon. When his father died a few years later, Matthew got an honorable discharge and came back to run it. He did that for two years and then sold the business. "It was hard," he says. "People didn't have jobs, and the only time they could pay was when an unemployment check arrived, and I didn't like being a bill collector."

He and Jackie were married while he was running the oil station, and then he left and went to work on the pipeline for two years. After that they went down south to the state of Washington to go to college, and then they came back to Angoon.

Matthew and Jackie have made one trip to New York City, which was paid for by a boatbuilding company on Long Island interested in knowing Matthew's ideas about boats. When they left Angoon, they brought some salmon on ice, as a gift for the people they were seeing. Matthew had planned to keep it in the freezer of the hotel, but the hotel wouldn't allow it, so he filled up his bathtub with ice and kept the fish there. He ended up with an extra fish. In the hotel dining room he found himself one morning seated near Muhammad Ali, and he tried to give him the fish, but Muhammad Ali said that he was on his way to France and couldn't take it.

Matthew knows the daughter of the last shaman in

Angoon. Several years ago, when he had his first fishing boat, someone told her that Matthew had fallen off of it. She came to him to tell him that there were certain things that he must do to protect himself against this, and even though it turned out that he hadn't fallen off, he gathered devil's club and a few other ingredients and boiled them together and used the potion to wash down the hull.

I SPENT enough time in Angoon that I became familiar to most people there, mainly because I walked everywhere I went and they saw me from their windows or passed me in their cars, or I talked to them or saw them at a basketball game or a food sale or at the store or the school or the harbor or the church. People who would probably recognize my name or know me by sight:

Joe Evans, a logger. He and his wife live a few doors from Matt, and I met him one morning when I had been to see Matt and he wasn't home and I saw Joe standing by the side of the road looking out at an eagle on a rock in the inlet. I had noticed him on occasion when he was walking to the boat harbor, and wondered who he was, because there weren't many white people around. He invited me into his house and I met his wife, who is Tlingit, and we drank coffee. Joe sat on the floor with his shoes off, and his wife sat on a couch against the picture window framing the house across the street and the inlet behind her. The television was on and it was dark enough in the room that the part of the couch in front of the TV was a different color from the rest. Joe said that about twenty-five years ago he had served as chief of police in Kake, another Tlingit town, not because he had any interest in being a policeman, but because he was logging then too, and was in terrific shape and could beat up everyone in town. At the time there was no such thing as a search warrant, he said, and it was important to be tough. He said that he really can't stand it down south, meaning in the state of Washington, because after he has been there for a while the congestion of roads and houses and traffic and people begins to feel as if it is closing in on him. What he likes in Alaska is that if he decides to settle an argument with his fists, he won't end up in jail. He said that his current plans were for him and his wife to sail their boat to places they had never been, and live off clams and fish, and then come back to Angoon and build a Victorian house out at Killisnoo. He had grown so tired of living in the small Indian houses and in logging camps and on sailboats that all he wanted was to live in a house with enough room so that he could have a corner with nothing in it but a table with a flower in a vase.

A woman who told me that a few years back she had been living in a trailer in the upper part of town and watching "The Price Is Right" one afternoon in her living room when a bear began to climb through a window in the kitchen. She really wanted to see who won, but she could also see the bear from where she was sitting. It had got so far into the room that a neighbor who observed it from outside told her later that all you could see of the bear were its hindquarters sticking out of the window. The woman had a cookie jar on a counter by the window, and the bear put one arm around the jar and the other inside it, and that was when she ran. She told me that the cannery sometimes had bear drills, the way they have fire drills other places.

George Paul, who was knocking down the remains of a burned-up house on the rocks along the inlet just below Matt's house and throwing the wood onto a fire on the beach. The house, which he had grown up in and lived in with his wife, had burned earlier in the winter, and each day he was coming down to the water and building a fire and banging down what was left of the walls and the foundation and the beams and the floor and burning them up to clear out the site. You could hear his hammer at work from a long way off; there were times when it was the only sound in town. The smoke from the fire drifted over the rooftops and joined the smoke from the chimneys of the houses still standing. At night the fire was glowing embers in the darkness on the rocks. When the work was done, he would join his wife in Barrow, on the north coast of Alaska, where she had got a job writing grants for the city. Someone had offered him a lot of money for the land, but he had turned it down. His intention was to stay two years in Barrow and make enough money to return to Angoon and rebuild. He already had his plans drawn up. The new house would be more substantial. The old one had been floated over from Killisnoo, which is what accounted for its placement beside the water. The climate in Barrow is forbidding, and he wasn't looking forward to going there, but the money his wife made and the possibilities for him made it difficult to turn down the opportunity. In Angoon he had a town job driving heavy equipment and grading the road, but it was seasonal work, and in the winter he drew unemployment. What he hoped to do when he got back was buy a boat and get into the gill-net fishery up in Haines. He pointed his hammer across the inlet to a small rocky piece of the shore where he had seen a bear walking in the fall. In the calm water on the other side of Village Rock, he said, his father would catch salmon on the change of the tide. Killer whales, seals, and sea lions chased herring up the inlet on the tide. Otters slid down the far bank. He said, "See those birds? They're here all year round." I asked what they were and he said,

"I don't know. Some kind of duck. I don't know what they are, we're so used to them we don't know their names." We spoke on the day of his last fire. A few days later I was walking around town and I saw him come out the door of a house and lock it and walk to his car in the driveway and throw a tarp over it, then get into a truck being driven by a friend who was taking him to the ferry terminal to catch the boat out.

Two girls from a teaching college in the Midwest who had come to Angoon for several weeks to work as interns in the school. To save money, they had arrived by ferry and brought with them seventy-six pounds of canned food in a trunk, because someone had told them it was expensive to shop in the store. What they were there for, they said, was to broaden themselves. "We won't always have just white people in our classrooms," one of them told me. I met them at a lunch held in the senior citizens center. For seven dollars you got two choices from a menu consisting of venison stew, smoked deer, cockles and rice, smoked salmon, seaweed, and salmon eggs. One of the teachers had promised to bring a smoked turkey. He was very late and the girls were waiting with empty plates, having no interest in Indian food.

Matsu Samato, who took me to see the remains of the cannery at Hood Bay. His ancestors are Japanese and Tlingit, and he and Matt grew up together. Matt's best friend was Matsu's brother Billy, who was killed in a fight in a bar in a southern port town while serving in the Navy. Matsu and three brothers and five sisters and their mother and father had lived at the cannery during the summer after it burned, while the company was shipping out what remained of the machinery and fish traps.

It was January and cold, and Matsu had just put up a cover, like a little pilothouse, on the deck of his Boston whaler. He had to do that, he said, or no one would go out with him anymore because of lack of protection from the cold and the wind. What gets cold first in a boat are your feet; Matsu touched only the outside of the sole of one of his to the deck and put the other on top of it and I copied him. We left the inlet, turned around the point, and came back past the cemetery and along the outside of town. What I thought was a reef in the distance came closer and turned out to be a school of porpoise, who torpedoed their long, dark, blurred shapes under us and then alongside for a while. Matsu said they were naturally curious and always checked boats heading into the bay. On the shore were a horizontal line of brown for the sand on the beach, a line of white above it for the snow, then a wall of green for the forest. There was snow and ice on the bow of the boat.

In Hood Bay were the remains of eighteen cabins alongside the water, and, where the cannery had stood, a rotting barge and some pilings with clams, and mussels, and seaweed clinging to them. Four ducks pinwheeled across the cove. It warmed our feet to walk. Some of the cabins were slanting toward the water or falling over. People from Angoon had scavenged the roofs. In nearly all of them you could see the sky through the rafters. In the woods above were more cabins, almost completely fallen down and covered by the forest. Matsu pointed up the hillside and said, "I lived in the next to last house up there. You can't see it now for the trees." We looked into the superintendent's house, which had the best work-manship, and I could see the walls stripped of wainscoting in about exactly the proportions that I remembered in place in Matt's house. Inside the superintendent's house Matsu found a bench, made from planks, and decided to take it back to town.

The seaweed along the tide line was frozen, and there were little rusty pieces of metal in it. Matsu said a boardwalk had run along the shore, connecting the houses. No trace of it was left.

On the way back the hills and the shoreline slid past like scenery passing the window of a train. Avalanche scars in the shape of arrows and sawteeth patterned the sides of some of the hills. Matsu pointed out a deer feeding on kelp at the tide line and occasionally raising his head to watch us. With Matsu saying, "Over there, right in line with the tree, see the branch by the rock, now sight straight down," I eventually found him. He said that when he hunts deer from the water he goes forward as slowly as he can, to keep down the noise. The deer stand still as a piece of furniture. Their bodies blend with the color of the beach. What he looks for is the white fur on the inside of the ears. He said that the place to look is not on the beach, but up in the forest where the woods and the beach meet, or at the kelp line. It was popular a few years ago to use binoculars, but then everyone began to realize they were looking at every detail, and it became maddening, so they went back to using their eyes. He said that by this time of the winter the deer have heard a lot of boats and got smarter from having been hunted so much. He said that you are not supposed to shoot deer from a boat but that some hunters do. The period of hunting deer when it is not legal is called the gunny sack season.

We slid across the bay, putting up ducks and watching them make wide, skidding turns in front of us. From Hood Bay we went back around the town and into the inlet and then up inside it. Some ways back into it we saw a rock on which were two crosses, and Matsu said that they were there to mark the death of two of Matt's relatives—one of his aunts and her daughter. They were on a seine boat, and the child was lost overboard and the mother went in to save her. Matsu intended to take me up into the salt lake where salmon spawn and a lot of people from Angoon do their fishing, but the tide was too low for us to make it over a rapids by the mouth of the lake. We anchored nearby and walked along the shore and followed some deer tracks in the snow for a while, then passed the rapids and walked along the shore of the lake. We found a seine rolled up and left for the next year's fishing and a campsite, and then we turned around and got back in the boat. Hills ran down alongside us like stair rails. We crossed the inlet with the sky going dark all around and the deer coming out on the beaches to feed.

I ARRIVED in Angoon with an introduction to Matthew Fred, who calls himself Chief of All Chiefs. Not usually in front of any other Tlingits, at least not ones from Angoon, but they have all read the statement in the paper at some time or another, or heard it from someone who has, and got angry over it and stored it away as a grievance. It is perhaps the first resentment a person encounters in Angoon. Matthew Fred is shrewd and engaging and generous and talkative, not to mention interested in everyone else's affairs, and it was natural that he would come to a position of authority in the town. On the wall in his office Matthew has a picture of himself on a stage in the East Room of the White House with President Carter and others, and it is signed "With Best Wishes to Chief Matthew Fred & the Tlingits of Admiralty Island, Jimmy Carter." Admiralty Island was made a National Monument in 1978, and on that occasion several people from Angoon went to Washington to meet Jimmy Carter, and it was apparently during this trip that Matthew began to suggest that the appropriate form of address for his person was "Chief of All Chiefs." Matthew claims his title as a consequence of his status as an elder in the raven beaver clan, the town's largest, and he qualifies it by saying that the designation applies only to Admiralty Island. Nevertheless, few in Angoon outside his family support it.

People in Angoon have met a lot of anthropologists and archaeologists and journalists of all kinds and have no real reason to talk to any of them, especially because it usually means time lost on other projects, and so I heard from a lot of people that they were too busy to see me, or didn't want to talk, or said come back some other time, mentioning then a time when they knew they wouldn't be home, and all this was frustrating until I discovered by accident a way to get their attention. I would call someone and ask for an interview and be turned down, and then I would pause, perhaps sigh, and say, "Well that's too bad, because I've been talking to Matthew Fred and—"

*"You've been talking to Matthew Fred?* Well, then you better get over here and hear the truth."

When I told Matthew that someone had challenged something he had told me, he would just get angry that I had questioned anything he said, and even angrier that I had talked about anything that concerned him to someone he considered a social inferior. About one person he said, "He lies with a completely straight face." About another, "There are nothing but lies in his house."

Matthew Fred is slight and wiry and about five feet ten inches tall. His face is square and deeply lined. He has a straight, wide mouth, and small, black, watery, and wide-set eyes. The most prominent feature of his face is a scar on his upper lip, which he received one night in a bar. He is a musician and for a while during the 1950s and 1960s made part of his living playing jazz in bars around

Juneau. He played the trumpet and taught himself to improvise from a correspondence course. "How I got to be a musician," he says, "I was hostile to white men, and I felt I could be just as good as them and do what they could do, and music was the way I felt I could do it." Some of the time, he double-jobbed, doing carpentry, or plumbing, or painting apartments, or laying tile. For a while he worked at a sawmill. While he did, he played music only on weekends, usually for Indian dances, because it was too dangerous to show up tired at the mill. Otherwise, he would play until one in the morning, come home and sleep until seven, get up and go to his day job, then come home and nap before leaving to play again. He played mainly at roadhouses and clubs. He played at the Occidental; he played at a place called Dream Land; he played the Bubble Room of the Baranof Hotel; and he played the L&L, which is where his lip got split. He was playing with his eyes closed, and a logger who didn't like Indians stepped up and slammed the bell of the trumpet back toward his face. The cut took six stitches. After that, Matthew switched to saxophone and played in a band called the Rhythm Chiefs, which also worked the Occidental.

Matthew grew tired of his life and of the kinds of people he met in bars. "That kind of life lost all its glory for me," he says. "I felt I didn't belong where I was at. It felt artificial. The kids weren't happy, and all the people in the barrooms could offer was the friendship of the bottle. Some people from Angoon came to see me and said they wanted me back home, and I began to think that if I kept up with it, where I would end up is dead someplace, overdosed, like most jazz musicians.

"I fished when I came home. Worked as a cook on a boat, then became a deck boss for a boat purse-seining, cracked the whip. In between that I would do subsistence. Then was a head maintenance man at a fish company, then a social worker, then water-and-sewer man for the town, then went into hospital for a stomach operation." Now he is the forestry-service boss on Admiralty, which is a seasonal job. He continues to play music, mostly guitar now, and mostly at church. He attends every church in Angoon.

I never felt more like a white guy than when I talked to Matthew Fred. The Tlingit appreciation of passing time is local and historical. There are the legends of their ancestors, which occur in a past that is not locatable, and there are the events in the history of where they live and in their clans that took place a long time ago and that no one really remembers exactly the same way from clan to clan and almost never from place to place, and then there are events of modern history, which also float in time, depending on who is recalling them. All of these forms of history have influenced Matthew Fred's sense of time. So much of Tlingit culture was destroyed by missionaries, but when I listen to Matthew Fred talk I sometimes think that one thing they never got their hands on was the Tlingit sense of time. An answer from Matthew to a question I asked never really seemed related to it in a way I could figure out. A question seemed as if it were an occasion for him to talk about whatever was on his mind. He would answer a simple question at some length, or by laboring over details, or with the recitation of a legend, the meaning of which was completely opaque to me, and I would always get impatient and end up wishing I had never asked him in the first place and trying to think of whom else I might go to to get the same information, and the answer, I think, was no one, because Matthew of all the elders has spent the most time with white people and is the most interested in conversation. The other elders I talked to were even more interior in the structure of their talk, or elusive, or private, or deep in the self-absorption of old age.

THE reason an American can go to a Tlingit village and understand what the people are saying and may, if he has done a little reading, know more about Tlingit tribal life in the past than do the Indians who live there, probably has a lot to do with the Presbyterians. The first missionaries into Alaska represented the Russian Orthodox Church. The Indians liked ritual and display, the showy interiors of the Orthodox churches, the fancy, imperial-looking gilded robes and jewels on the priest, the burning of incense, and the mysteries of a long, chant-filled service carried on in an impenetrable tongue. Attending church also offered the Indians the chance to dress up.

Presbyterian missionaries arrived in 1877. The Russian missionaries did not care for card-playing, or wine-drinking, or slander, or argument, or shamans, or the Indian memorial parties called potlatches, or any kind of spirit worship other than their own, but otherwise they endorsed the way the Tlingit lived their lives and did not try to civilize them according to ideas brought from home. The Presbyterians considered the culture of the Tlingit to be backward, brutal, and repellent. Here is a Russian Orthodox missionary describing the Tlingit language: "Their speech is flowery and rich in imagery, and they are generally good orators. . . . The language itself is rich with words but even richer in grammatical forms. Nouns and adjectives have articles, as in Greek; persons, tenses, and moods of nouns and adjectives are modified by means of prefixes. . . . Listening carefully to the speech of a Tlingit, you might hear the croaking of a frog, the bubbling of water, the cackling of a hen, the crackle of breaking dry wood, or some guttural and rather pleasant, melodious sounds." And here is a Presbyterian: "The sooner . . . the natives drop their stunted and dwarfed language for the liberal English, the better. No encouragement to hold on to their language should be given by missionaries and teachers learning it with the view of addressing them in it. The best way of elevating them is to make them climb up to us."

The Presbyterians opened schools, in which they forbade the children to speak their own language. A missionary at one beat two girls who came to school wearing snowshoes. The reason he gave for the beating was that while there was no scriptural prohibition against snowshoes, there was no scriptural authority for them either. Snowshoes were the invention of the heathen, and the missionary believed that Indian girls ought to report to school through the snow like Christian and civilized women. The girls ran away and were caught and brought back. To rid themselves of Presbyterian missionaries the entire Indian population of Killisnoo once requested baptism in the Orthodox Church.

Nevertheless, the Orthodox Church was in decline, and the Presbyterian advanced, particularly in Sitka. Some of the converts were drawn by the novelty and the hope of acquiring power by learning to pray and sing in the Protestant fashion.

At the head of the Presbyterian Church in Alaska was a missionary named Sheldon Jackson. Unlike the Orthodox missionaries, who felt that the Tlingit ought to be encouraged toward God without giving up their way of living from the sea and the forest, Jackson had an idea that the Indians should be taught to herd reindeer and to become farmers, with the intention of providing cheap food and transportation and labor for the European and American immigrants. Jackson believed that a teacher should be a married man and that a well-run household was a lesson to the Indians. His goal was to instill in the Indians as "their highest ambition ... to build American homes, possess American furniture, dress in American clothes, adopt the American style of living, and be American citizens."

Many Tlingit wanted their children to learn to read and write so as to be able to compete with white people, but they resented the school's forced attendance, the ban on speaking Tlingit, and the attacks on potlatches, shamanism, and other of their beliefs. Also, they began to realize that being Presbyterian did not protect them from discrimination or necessarily give them a respectable position. White men, often other Presbyterians, still took their lands.

The Presbyterian church in Angoon was built in 1923, the Russian Orthodox church in 1929, after the one in Killisnoo burned down. There are three other churches in Angoon: one belonging to the Salvation Army, one to the Assembly of God, and one that has no denomination. All except the Orthodox church have their own ministers. An Orthodox priest comes on a circuit from the mainland.

I went one night to the Assembly of God because Matthew Fred asked me to, and I thought perhaps it was a test and that if I didn't he wouldn't talk to me anymore. Also, I went because I thought I might find in the spectacle of a missionary preaching to the Indians something to make fun of. It started out pretty well. I had, in the minister, a red-haired guy from Kansas standing up and singing and leading everyone along as if it were a tent meeting somewhere in the South, and shouting "Praise

Jesus" at unpredictable moments, like some kind of hill-
billy, and with a beatific smile on his face that I found
unconvincing, and then people began to stand up and talk
about their experience of the work of the Lord in their
lives, what is called testifying, and invariably some of what
they said was trivial—a woman, for example, who felt the
Lord had seen to it that her son broke his ankle in a basketball game as a lesson—but then I heard George Paul
talk about leaving town and going to Barrow, and a
woman about a horrible and serious operation she faced
that would be painful and frightening and leave her with
little hope of long life, and someone else about a sickness,
and another about drinking, and the troubles just came
pouring out, and pretty soon it didn't feel so amusing,
and I began to feel humiliated and ashamed in myself at
having thought that I ever might find something comical
in other people's troubles and desperate reasons for faith,
and I put my notebook away and sat there and sang the
songs when they came up, and thought that whatever else
I or anyone else thinks about the Tlingit and the myths
they know and the culture they brought into being and
its artifacts, they are also now regular Americans, and the
triumph of Sheldon Jackson is complete, and the catalogue
of adversaries that attack people leading lives they hope
to be good and happy and well protected is fierce and
relentless and mean and low-down and gets everyone
everywhere.

IN the canoe days, the Tlingit called God a high-up rich
man. They would sometimes invite their enemies to a feast,
then in the middle of it murder them. To lure Europeans
ashore for an ambush a Tlingit might dress in a bearskin
and walk up and down the beach. Americans the Tlingit

called Boston men, and the British, King George men. Indians in Canada they called King George Indians. The Tlingit thought white people smelled bad, especially Russians. White people other than Russians the Tlingit called People from the Place Where the Clouds Reach Down to the Earth, that is, the horizon.

The Tlingit began to wear beards and mustaches after meeting white men; before that they had usually plucked the hair from their faces. They also began to put doors on their houses, and, around 1900, to use chairs, but tables were less common. Before white men, the Tlingit would leave their villages for months at a time without making provisions for protecting their property. Sometimes they would leave a house in the village open for strangers.

Some Tlingit thought twins were an omen of evil, others that they were lucky, and others that they occurred from having had sex on consecutive nights. A sick Tlingit finding a bug on himself believed he would die from his illness. Widows were not to eat boiled fish, or else their heads would come loose and flop from side to side. A mother would capture her child's first cries in a bag and then carry it to a place where people were passing, so that it would be walked on, in order to keep the child from crying too much.

When a Tlingit loaned money he expected twice the amount back. Tlingit trading parties always took with them an old woman to do their bargaining, because they believed old women to be shrewder. The Tlingit had no expression for "thank you." White people thought they were ungrateful. A Tlingit man once came to the door of the doctor of his village to beg for medicine for his brother, then demanded money to carry it. Samuel H. Young, the Presbyterian missionary in Wrangell in the late nineteenth century, wrote about caring for a sick Indian for more than a year in a room within the fort. "My wife and I tended and nursed him as if he were a brother," he wrote. "We expended upon him more than a hundred dollars in medicine, food and clothing. After he had recovered in some degree and was able to return to his home and do some work, I found him standing by his canoe on the beach one day and said, 'Charlie, I wish you would take me in your canoe over to Shustack's Point,' half a mile distant. He looked at me for a moment and then said, 'How much you going to pay me?' 'Have you no shame?' I asked. 'Have you forgotten all that I have done and spent for you the past year?'

"He eyed me with a look that made me want to knock him over. 'That's your business,' he said in Tlingit. 'My canoe is my business.' "

A Tlingit man who had received a serious insult would go back to his clan house and say, "I was insulted by," and give the name, and add, "I am going to die." Then he would arm himself and prepare to kill or be killed. This kind of killing would never be done from ambush. In one Tlingit village two men got into a quarrel. One was sick. The well one came to the sick man's house to settle the argument. Since he could not stand, the sick man had the other sit on a box. They began to stab each other until they passed out. When they revived they started up again until both were dead.

The Tlingit boiled water not over a fire but by tossing heated rocks into it. Sometimes Tlingit would put ear wax on their kindling to start a fire. Tlingit had no regular mealtimes, instead they ate whenever they felt like it. Eating beach food—that is, cockles, clams, mussels, sea urchins, crabs, and seaweed—at night was thought to cause nightmares and bad weather.

Each Tlingit believed he had a guardian spirit which

stayed close to him, usually above his head, and left him only at death or when he committed a serious crime.

The Tlingit thought that all rocks, animals, trees, plants, stars, planets, and the sun were alive and had the same thoughts and feelings and passions and needs as they did, only were generally more cunning and powerful. They believed that owls could speak Tlingit and predict the weather; before a storm owls were thought to be saying, "Get under trees." Owls were also believed able to identify murderers, so sometimes they were shot. Animals of all kinds were thought able to understand human speech, therefore the Tlingit were especially careful never to say anything insulting about bears. A bear's main attributes were thought to be generosity, pride, honesty, and vengefulness. Also, a bear is able to feel shame. It was believed that a male bear would run away from a naked woman, so sometimes when Tlingit women met a bear in the forest they would take off their clothes.

The Tlingit were fond of tattooing young women. The color of the design would be pricked in using a needle, or else a thread soaked in dye would be drawn through the skin. Their favorite colors were red and blue, then black. A common woman could have a vertical line in the center of her chin and one parallel to it on either side. A higher-class woman was allowed two long vertical lines from the corners of her mouth.

Tlingit society had four levels: those of the highest caste, then people of no distinction, then low-class nobodies, then slaves. A Tlingit man coming to a town where he knew no one was not supposed to speak until someone spoke to him. Beyond that, it was felt that only a nobody would talk a lot, as a means of drawing attention, so a high-caste person visiting a town where he wasn't known would be careful not to say too much.

A wealthy man might pay two slaves or eight blankets for a wife for his son.

Some Tlingits believed that long ago the whole world spoke Tlingit, but that the Lord then confused the tongues of the other nations, and the Tlingits alone retained their speech.

The Tlingit thought the earth was flat. In the winter they spent a lot of time gambling, mainly playing guessing games and throwing chair dice—that is, dice carved in the shape of a chair, solid and flat on two sides, with six edges.

When the Tlingits became Christians and married, the wedding announcement would refer to the bride as a maid of the forest. Sometimes a Tlingit would meet a white man and ask him to tell everything he knew about God. They would sometimes commit suicide by taking to sea in a canoe with no paddle.

When a Tlingit left on a long journey, his friends watched him out of sight for fear he might never return.

FIGHTING a battle on the water, a Tlingit tribe once chopped off the hands of its enemies so that they couldn't swim home. In combat the Tlingit wore armor made from wooden staves and helmets carved in the image of monsters. Beforehand, they painted their faces black to hide any fear and because black was the color of death. It was their custom to attack at night. A Russian describing a raid said that the Indians were able to crawl within ten feet of his soldiers before beginning their attack. "In that darkness," he wrote, "they seemed more terrifying to us than the most awful devils of hell." Once the battle was under way a certain number of warriors would approach in formation, while others ran back and forth. Sometimes when they rushed into battle they would hoot like owls.

The Tlingits were the only tribe of Northwest Indians to take scalps. When they did, they took the ears also. What they valued most was the scalp of a white woman. During wars they took slaves and used them later to do their housework. The Flathead Indians of British Columbia were the tribe the Tlingit most often struck for slaves. The Tlingit liked slaves from far away, because it was harder for them to escape. In Angoon, during the nineteenth century, the value of a slave was thirty fox skins, ten moose skins, two marten-skin blankets, and one Chilkat blanket. Women were the same price, less ten fox skins. Dead slaves were never buried, but were dragged to the beach and thrown into the water and left for the tide to take away.

One of the reasons the Tlingit attacked at night was that they knew they would be held responsible by a victim's relatives if they were caught. One of the American naval commanders in Sitka at the end of the last century wrote that fear of consequences reduced all the Tlingit wars to "secret assassinations, except when through liquor they become imprudent."

As it did elsewhere, the rifle in Alaska changed Indian wars forever. The Tlingit feared white men with rifles sufficiently that by the end of the nineteenth century the sight of a steam launch approaching was enough to empty a whole village.


B Y the time people got around to taking pictures of them, the Tlingit wore European clothes. Groups of men would sit in a photographer's studio and hold a pose with expressions that can be read as sullen or grave or backward or resentful or churlish or somber or something else entirely: how could anyone know. Or a shaman would be persuaded to dress in the skins he wore for his ceremonies and to hold some of his rattles in his hands and stand beside a few of his charms: the look on his face suggests he is familiar with some aspects of magic and is not even close to comfortable with the idea of what kind the man under the sheet behind the lens might be using. Or a group of women would come into the studio and put on some robes and sit in front of things they had made to sell to the tourists who came off the boat at Juneau or Sitka. In any picture of more than four or five people, there is more than one type of face, but nearly all have high cheekbones, and dark eyes, and black hair, prominent, looming foreheads and brows, and mouths that turn down at the corners. The men tended not to be tall and often were bowlegged, which the Europeans said came from spending so much time kneeling in canoes. The women as they aged grew stout; some are described as weighing three hundred and fifty pounds.

To show anger at an insult the Tlingit painted their faces black, using charcoal. To protect themselves against burns from the sun and the wind, as well as against mosquitoes, cold, and snow blindness, the glare off the water, and the heat of the open fire they covered their faces with a concoction made from a variety of ingredients such as spruce gum, soot, graphite, deer fat, goat fat, and seal grease. The mixture dried hard and was waterproof and lasted for weeks. High-caste women also covered their faces with powders and pastes to bleach their complexions. The Tlingit had an abhorrence of any damage to the face. A wound on the face was shameful and had to be paid for by the person who caused it. In fighting they almost always struck only the body.

Some doctors believed that the Tlingit's constitution

was much stronger than the white man's and that the Tlingit required twice the amount of medicine as the white man to produce the same effect. They were said not to notice wind or rain or cold. A Tlingit who was going to ford a river would take off his clothes and sit down in the water for a while. At night they would sleep so near to the fires that they came close to burning, while on the other side of their bodies would be frost.

As for their bearing, this was written by someone who visited Alaska in the nineteenth century: "The raggedest old man in the village, when talking with a white man, will draw his blanket around him with the air of a monarch. As one of them once said, 'The earth is a round ball, and the white man is on top now and the Indians underneath; but some day the ball will roll over, and it will be the Indians' turn to be on top.' "

THE Russians called the Tlingit the Kaloch, which they also spelled Kalosch, Kolosch, and Kaljusch. A doctor at the Russia America Company wrote, "The Kaloches are proud, egoistic, revengeful, spiteful, false, intriguing, avaricious, love above all independence, and do not submit to force, except the ruling of their elders." A Presbyterian missionary in the nineteenth century described the Tlingit as industrious, hardy, and brave, adding that he "sails the deep in frail and cranky canoes, scours the forest for ferocious animals, and often meets his human antagonist without fear." The Tlingits hated working for anyone and couldn't stand being bossed. Tlingit girls hired as servants in the morning frequently disappeared by the afternoon. The Tlingit liked the ceremonial importance of military dress and often joined the Salvation Army so that they could wear the uniform. They were touchy and thin-skinned and sensitive to insults and ridicule and shame. Schoolteachers noted that their children learned quickly.

A German travelling in the nineteenth century wrote that when a Tlingit finished his work of the day he would find a rocky point on a beach and sit there, wrapped in a blanket, without moving, sometimes for hours. The Russians at Sitka were familiar with a particular rock that the Indians favored. A Norwegian anthropologist writing in 1932 noted that in the Tlingit villages he went to he often found men just sitting around, and that it was common for several to sit together in a room for hours and not say anything. He said one would walk into another's house and sit there for a while and get up and leave without having said a word. He also said that he would see men early in the morning just walking around on the beach or the hillsides near the town. If he asked them what they were doing, they said just looking around. He concluded that the Indian did not know what to do with his spare time.

Aurel Krause, the German traveller, said that the Tlingit were fond of letters of recommendation from Europeans and would collect them and bring them out to impress others. One chief used to show around a letter that said he owed a company for tobacco and another that said he was known to have a weakness for making love to white women.

Other observations. A naval commander, nineteenth century: "The Thlinkets are a hardy, self-reliant, industrious, self-supporting, well-to-do, warlike, superstitious race, whose very name is a terror to the civilized Aleuts to the west, as well as to the savage Tinneh to the north of them."

A military man, also nineteenth century: "Like all Indians, however brave, they are mortally afraid of cannon, Gatling guns, and any other large arms not used by themselves, and a single well-directed shell would have more moral effect and less fatal results in bringing them to terms than a village full of corpses produced by weapons with which they are familiar and can meet man for man, gun for gun."

The same man said that the houses in Angoon were, as a rule, absolutely bulletproof, "but would necessarily be abandoned if the attacking force were provided with the lightest forms of artillery."

THE first European to trade with the Tlingit, toward the end of the eighteenth century, was Jean François de Galaup La Pérouse, a French navigator. He wrote that they stole anything they could get their hands on. They tore the iron fittings loose from his ship. They tried to sneak aboard at night. He would invite the headmen onto the ship and give them gifts, and they would steal a nail or an old sock. Whenever he noticed them smiling, he was sure that they had stolen something. He gave orders that presents were to be given to the children, in hopes of winning the parents' good will, but whenever his crew were busy with the children, he would notice one or another of the fathers stealing something. When they were caught they were not ashamed, but only embarrassed at not carrying it off.

Traders at Sitka in the early nineteenth century would close off the forward part of the ship with sails to the height of a man. Behind the sails would stand an armed crew alongside cannons loaded with grapeshot. Around the deck the traders would string a net that had only one entrance, wide enough for one person. Before trading began, they would bring the chiefs on board and tell them that only a certain number of Indians would be allowed on the ship at one time. None would be allowed more than ten feet from the rails, and if anyone was killed for violating these rules it should not be considered an event worthy of breaking a peace.

Although traders describe them as dishonest, their relations among themselves were always marked by truthfulness and respect for property. The Tlingit considered a person who stole to be under a spell.

EVENTUALLY, from someone in Juneau, I learned that the inscription on the T-shirt referred to the shelling of Angoon by the American Navy, who felt that the Hootsnoowoos had become dangerous and were threatening the white settlement at Killisnoo and needed to be put down, but the person who told me about it said that it would not be a good idea to raise the subject with the people in Angoon, who were still upset about it.

ALL five kinds of Pacific salmon—humpback, dog, sockeye, coho, and king—reside in the waters around Angoon. All except king spawn in streams on the island.

In past times the Tlingit believed that salmon lived in houses under the sea in a place far away and in appearance were more or less like people, and that they observed much the same customs and manners as the Tlingit. Each year they assumed the shapes of salmon and travelled across the ocean to the streams and rivers that belonged to the Tlingit. As long as their bones were returned to the water the salmon would come back. Because salmon were so abundant in their streams and rivers, the Tlingit never developed a first-salmon ceremony, like other Northwest Coast Indians. In first-salmon ceremonies, the Indians would greet the first salmon to arrive as if it were a chief paying a visit and address speeches to it and throw a party for it.

The Tlingit would stand on rocks in the streams and spear salmon with spears made from cedar, or shoot them with bows and arrows, or during the winter build weirs and traps, or sharpen stakes and set them in the mud of the flats so that salmon leaping rapids would fall back on the stakes.

Some of the salmon they ate fresh, most of it they smoked. They were fond of something called stinkheads, salmon heads wrapped in skunk cabbage and buried several days in a barrel below the tide line. They liked salmon best just before the fish spawned, when they had used up most of their body fat, so they would dry better.

What is called the seasonal round—that is, the activities of the harvest that begin in the summer and continue through the cycle of the year—starts in early summer, with the arrival of the salmon. The first to show up in the waters around Angoon is the sockeye. It arrives in mid-June or early July and lasts into August. Next to arrive is the pink, also called the humpback or the humpy, because of the grotesque changes the male undergoes during spawning. When humpbacks arrive at the fresh water the males look like normal salmon, then the bones in their foreheads spread apart until they are wider by a third, and their snouts get longer by two-thirds. The hump that they grow on their backs increases their height by almost a quarter. The dog salmon, also called the chum, follows the pink and arrives in two runs; summer dogs in late June and fall dogs in September. Cohos show up in Angoon in late September.

The return of the salmon coincides with that of creatures that rely on the salmon for food. Crab, halibut, seals, and trout return to the bays to prey on the salmon that have finished spawning and are dying, and also on their eggs.

During the summer and up until the first frost, deer live in the open meadows above the timber line. You can see them from a distance, dark against the background of green. Hunters reach them by bear trails. Late summer and into the fall is also the time for the harvest of wild fruit—thimbleberries, huckleberries, salmonberries, and blueberries. In October the Tlingit begin taking seals. Mostly they get them in the bays on the rocks and reefs where they rest and at the mouths of salmon streams. Most are taken by chance during the course of a deer trip. By October deer have moved to the muskegs and low woods. Hunters hope for snow by the first of December to force them to the beaches. Clams, cockles, gumboots, chitins, and sea cucumbers comprise the winter harvest. In the last of February Dolly Varden trout arrive at the mouths of the salmon streams to feed on the fry of the chum and humpback salmon leaving mostly at night for open water. In March the herring return to spawn. The Tlingit cut hemlock branches and leave them in the water for the eggs of the herring to collect on. In April the Tlingit collect two kinds of seaweed—black and red ribbon—and dry it to use later in stews and, in the case of the black, to cook up with salmon eggs. In May, when the seals are having their pups, the Tlingit leave off hunting them and don't start again until the fall.

Beach logging is carried on throughout the year. Logs are lost in Chatham Strait from barges on their way to the pulp company, or float away from log rafts, and either they drift in to shore and are found or someone in a boat out looking for them throws a rope around one and tows it to shore. Logs found above the high-water mark with the company brand are company property for ninety days. Firewood from logs that have been left on the beach is seasoned and contains less pitch, which is an advantage; a lot of house fires start in pitchy chimneys.

THE Tlingit in Angoon do not rely only on cash and they do not barter. They have what is called a mixed economy; it relies on cash to buy guns and fishing gear and whatever else they need to keep them in the business of finding food. In order for it to work there has to be a lot of wilderness around them to support the animals they rely on. Lately the main threats to the welfare of the town's economy have been logging and the promise of quick cash. A lot of the woods around Tlingit communities have been logged. The Indians sold the rights and got the money and bought pickup trucks and for a while seemed better off. One of the reasons Angoon has been called the last outpost of Tlingit culture is that the people who live there have held on to their preference for fresh Indian food: that means they need the forest, and furthermore that they oppose logging. The Tlingit have traditionally believed that food can be acquired much faster than money, and that gathering food provides capital for trade.

The people of Angoon could have made a lot of money from logging. They could have had an airport and more roads, but they don't sell their land to outsiders. White people who have got hold of land around Angoon have usually managed to do it through a connection to the Forest Service or some other part of the government. It happens that there is a fairly high turnover of teachers in Angoon, and people in town say that one reason is that the town makes it difficult for teachers to buy land and build houses they can sell later for whatever price a vacation house in Alaska would bring. In this way the people who live in Angoon have kept the price of their land from rising beyond their means. They have been able to do so because of the Alaska Native Claims Settlement Act, put through in 1971, which gave holdings of land to local corporations to manage. Angoon has control over a little more than thirty-five hundred acres surrounding it. The Forest Service controls the rest. It was in this portion that white people were sometimes able to buy.

It is difficult for the Tlingit in Angoon to think of the land as an asset for profit, when they have traditionally considered themselves caretakers. They do not like the idea of profit or business in connection with the idea of land. "Standing on the beach" is a Tlingit phrase, and when they use it in discussions about land and about logging what they mean is that they can look down the road at a future based on logging, and not only do they see themselves losing their hunting grounds, but they also see themselves dispossessed of work, standing on the beach, watching white men at work in their forests.

The Tlingit feel that they have lived properly and with success from the land for thousands of years. They never hunted themselves out of anything. The white man shows up and it takes only a hundred years to have trouble with the forests and the game and the fish.

The Tlingit in Angoon know they are poor from stopping the logging. If they can't see it from looking at their lives and comparing what they own to the comforts of those of the Tlingit who have permitted logging and are now driving pickups, then those people tell them. The Tlingit in Sitka like to tell the ones in Angoon that they are stupid and don't know how to make money. The Tlingit in Angoon know that if they cut the timber, the game would leave. They have seen it in the places on the island where logging went on in past times. The forest grew back too thick, nothing can move in it; game shuns the area, the hunting is worthless. They see it in the communities where logging goes on and the wind blows over the bald, scarred-up, empty land. And anyway they wonder what would happen to the children born after the forest was gone.

Most of the money that is made in Angoon is made by fishermen fishing from small boats with hand-trolls. In 1982 there were five hundred and sixteen people living in town. The school system gave jobs to thirty of them, almost all of them white people from outside Angoon. Whatever business there was in the town, the store for example, and the offices of the government, gave jobs to thirty more. The store is expensive, and the meat is frozen. The majority of households use between one and fifteen deer in the course of a year, some use none, and some use as many as thirty. Nearly all the families eat shellfish that they dig for themselves or buy from another person in town or trade for or accept as a gift. The same goes for fish from the ocean, particularly salmon and halibut. In 1986 nearly half the people in Angoon made less than five thousand dollars for the year. Some made no money at all.

The demise of the fishing fleet began with the closing of the cannery at Hood Bay. The cannery was built in the nineteen-twenties and was bought by the town of Angoon in 1947, and in 1961 it burned up. No one knows exactly how the fire started; the explanation one sometimes hears is that the insurance wires got hot. The cannery bought fish and stored boats and lent money for repairs and new nets and food for trips, as well as for fishermen's funerals and doctors' bills. When it went out of business the fishermen could still sell their fish at other canneries, but there were none close at hand, and none that gave them the same favorable treatment. In 1975 the Angoon fishing fleet included fourteen boats, which were described in a Bureau of Indian Affairs report as "deteriorating," mainly because their owners were unable to raise money to take care of them. In 1974, Alaska began to control the number of fishing boats in its waters by means of permits issued to owners. A certain number were given out, and then the fishery was closed. Many of those owners who qualified for them in Angoon received theirs and then sold them for a few thousand dollars and used the money to buy smaller boats. Some sold them because they needed the money, and some because they had grown tired of fishing and all its new restrictions. They had begun to feel like the machine that pulls the fish from the water, and that all their knowledge of places to find fish and what they knew about the landscape of the grounds and the seasons and migrations came to matter next to nothing because the new way of fishing, which was to open a fishery for a limited amount of time, didn't take that into account. Under this new practice fishing seasons were called openings. The season could be as short as twenty-four hours, as is the case with halibut. Usually there are two, maybe three halibut openings a year, which gives a fisherman forty-eight or seventy-two hours to make his year's money on halibut. Another difficulty with openings is that it was no longer possible to make a living from pursuing one kind of fish; you now had to participate in several kinds of fishing, not only for salmon, but for black cod also, and for halibut, and whatever else you could find that was legal that would make you some money in between. The permits these days are worth many times what the people in Angoon got for them. At present, there are only three purse-seiners in Angoon, one of which belongs to a white man who has married into the town.

On the far end of the beach by the boat harbor are three derelict boats, the Junior, the Pan Alaska, and the Midnight Sun. Sickness or debt took them out of the fishery. Most of the glass in the windows of their pilothouses is broken. Snow drifts on their decks. The tide walks in and out underneath them. They tower above a person on the beach. Ravens stare down from their masts. Their owners sit home and watch television.

THERE is a story that is told in Angoon to illustrate the strife and tension of small-town tribal life. A white man is watching an Indian gather crabs on the beach. Every time the Indian gets a crab he puts it in a paper bag he has left on the rocks and goes off and gets another. The bag begins to fill up. The white man decides to do the same thing, but every time he puts a crab in his bag, it climbs out. He walks over to the Indian and says, "How come my crabs climb out of the bag, and when you put them in there they stay?" And the Indian says, "Oh, these are Indian crabs. Every time one of them tries to get ahead, the others all hold him back."

BECAUSE I asked him to, Matt Kookesh took me one morning past the high school and into the woods and along a path down to the beach, past a pile of rocks left by a man who was training to be a boxer and would pick up the rocks from the corners of the beach and carry them to the pile, and around a prominence at one end of the beach called Magpie Point and up to a small ledge in the side of a cliff to look at a painting I had heard about made there by Indians in former times. The painting is of a sailing ship, seen from the side. It is the red-brown color of a certain kind of rust. There are three masts, each of which has three yards, and each of which supports rigging but no sails. Between each mast, rising from the deck, is a vertical line; in proportion to the masts each line is about the height of a person, and it is possible that this is what they represent. The hull is outlined more than painted. A fine green moss grows within it. Other figures were painted beside the ship—one was of a face with a wide, grinning mouth full of teeth—but they have faded out entirely. Anthropologists have suggested that the painting was perhaps made to commemorate a wreck, or the first ship to be seen off Angoon, but no one really knows why or when or by whom it was made. Matt and I stood on the ledge where the painter stood, feeling his presence, then Matt turned and pointed with his chin out over the water and said, "The boat was probably moored right over there."

We climbed back down to the beach and I followed Matt farther up the shore, away from the town, and over some rocks and tidal pools until he stopped and pointed about twenty feet above us at a cut in the rock that was an entrance to a cave and said that a shaman was buried in it.

Matt wouldn't go any closer to the grave, and it was clear he didn't want to hang around it, so I followed him back up the path to where there was a fork with one trail leading back to the parking lot and the high school and one leading into the woods. He told me that the second branch led several miles through the forest to Killisnoo and that he would take it with me, but he had to get back to work, and I said, fine, I would take it by myself. He went back to town, and I walked a little way down the path and waited a moment, then circled back to the shaman's grave. I did not expect to see anything in it, because I knew that nearly every shaman who ever was buried has had his grave looted by white men, and that those in Angoon had been particularly hard hit, but I wanted to see it anyway. The cave led down into the rock and there were steps of a kind on one edge, which you could use by crouching and leaning to the side against one wall. I went down two of them, which was far enough to see the bottom, about five feet below. Resting on a log against the back wall was a skull, the sockets of its eyes facing the water Indian style, like beacons. I do not know the name of the shaman who is buried there, but later I learned that in the past the people in Angoon called his grave Small Spirit's House. They believed that if you spoke to him his spirit would answer, and that then you were supposed to say thank you.

I went back to the fork in the trail and took the long walk to Killisnoo. The woods were dark and damp and silent. I crossed muskegs and old, soft, lumpy moss-covered stumps of fallen spruce and hemlock and pine. The trees were tall and big around at the base and close together. What light broke through the tops of them fell here and there on their trunks like the light from a spotlight. Nearly all the way I had with me the sound of water running through streambeds in the forest, then falling onto rocks on the beach. The path was paved with needles from the trees; it gave like peat moss and crunched under my feet where frost had got into it. The underbrush grew so thickly alongside the trail that there was no leaving the path. On the right-hand side I could see the strait through breaks in the trees. Ravens called from the canopy and flew in the space between the top of the underbrush and the lowest of the branches. If I stayed still long enough they came closer a tree at a time and stared at me, then took off, pumping their wings and giving out a cry like a bulletin. Twice I took trails that played out because I had been watching the placement of my feet and had missed the marker and was vexed at losing my way so easily in the woods.

I passed the foundation and one leaning wall of an old cabin, then the path turned to the right and came out abruptly onto the beach at the water line. Straight ahead about fifty feet, with its back to me and staring at the water from a perch on a rock, was an eagle. It didn't know I was there, and I was starting to recover by thinking that if I ever wanted to, I could probably be a great tracker, then one of my goddamn, clumsy, used-for-walking-the-avenues feet cracked a stick, and the next thing I was looking at was an empty, vibrating place in the air, just above the surface of a rock, where there used to be an eagle.

FOUR   Tlingit songs, the first sung at a feast for the dead:

> I always compare you to a drifting log with iron nails in it. Let my brother float in, in that way. Let him float ashore on a good sandy beach.
> I always compare you, my mother, to the sun passing behind the clouds. That is what makes the world dark.

A song sung by wolf families on their way to a feast:

A rich man is coming. Your feelings you keep silent.
When it is ended, thus they always say, "It is all gone."

Song sung to a child in his cradle:

Let me shoot a small bird for my younger brother
Let me spear a small trout for my sister

Sung on the way to jail:

They sound like howling wolves from here
everybody just beginning to get drunk
& I have to go away

THE people in Angoon have a relationship with the white people who teach their children that is difficult and conflicted and demeaning. Some parents feel that the model in the mind of the person who hires their teachers is a married man, with young children, strong Christian religious convictions, and a wife who will be given a job in the school system. They sometimes feel they are suffering a second coming of the missionaries. There are native women in Angoon who are qualified to teach, have taught elsewhere, and wish for the positions that are given to some of the white teachers' wives. Angoon is not necessarily the first choice of young men and women who would like to teach in Alaska. It is said among the town that teachers with daughters tend to leave by the time the girls reach the eighth grade, because the teachers don't want them in a romance with an Indian.

In talking about the natives the white people often say how much they do for them, which, of course, implies ingratitude. A woman teacher who has been a certain number of years in Angoon told me that she and her husband had given up attending the Indian memorial parties. "We just stopped," she said. "They go on and on until two in the morning sometimes, and we just can't afford to give up that much of the next day. They're very disruptive." I said that I thought most of the parties were held on Saturday nights. "Even so," she said, "we just don't have time for it. They just ruin your next day. And then when it comes time for them to come to a party for a white person, they just don't even bother to show up." She mentioned the name of a man who had died and said, "They didn't even bother to come to his memorial, and after all he did for them. We tried, but we just had to give up."

The women in town feel that the women who work in the schools remain aloof, and some of the local women wonder why. It is known that some teachers have been warned away by their superiors from friendships with people in the town. Several years ago a schoolteacher's wife was raped by an Indian. Her husband was away in another part of the state. The Indian called her and said he had seen him and that the husband had given him a package for her. He suggested that the woman come to his house to pick it up. The man is in jail, and there is not a person anywhere in the town who would not wish the woman's experience undone, but some native women say that everyone in town knew that the guy was a problem, and had learned to avoid him, but the schoolteachers, by holding themselves apart, did not allow to take place the occasion on which they might have been told.

I WENT halibut fishing with Matt Kookesh. The opening was scheduled to begin at noon of the first day in May and last twenty-four hours. I moved back into the same room at the lodge, but took all my meals with Matt and Jackie. My first night I followed Matt into the yard and held open the door of the smokehouse while he cut steaks from a deer, and we had them with beans and carrots and, afterwards, blueberry pie with ice cream. We drank some beer and then, because it was April and not January, I walked home practicing in my mind lying down and looking dead to a bear, and then I got in bed and lay in the darkness listening to two Indian women standing upstairs on the balcony scream at each other about a man that both of them were seeing. One was more reasonable than the other, who was close to hysterical, and who said, "I'll kill you if you don't stay away," and I waited for the gun shot, and then the two of them started crying and the more reasonable one left.

The next morning Matt went to see if he could find any more octopus in the rocks on the beach along the strait, and Jackie and Nikolai and I went with him. Matt had an octopus hook made of a steel rod taken from a box spring. It was about as tall as he was and had a sharp filed hook turned up half a foot at one end. We walked past the Assembly of God church, down the embankment to the beach, then stopped to watch some ducks arrowing toward the strait. Beside us in the woods were birds that made sounds like police whistles. In Juneau, where I had stopped on my way to Angoon, I had walked in the woods, and the people there, blowing whistles to alert the bears, made it sound as if basketball games were being played all over the forest. We walked along the beach toward the small white crosses in the graveyard at the end of the point, Jackie and I each carrying buckets that joint compound had come in and Jackie also carrying Nikolai on her back. Matt walked along the edge of the water and sometimes into it, beyond the tide, working his hook into holes between the rocks. One way to get an octopus out of a hole he won't leave is to pour Clorox into it, or spit snuff, what Matt calls Indian tobacco, but you're not supposed to do either.

Chatham Strait was flat as a mirror. Someone had worked the beach a few tides earlier—there were tentacles left behind on some rocks by the water line—which made Matt wonder if he was wasting his time. I didn't have the right shoes for the water, so I stayed on the beach and gathered red ribbon seaweed off the rocks with Jackie, and watched Matt in the distance out at the edge of the tide line stick his hook into a hole and jerk it back and flip an octopus up and into the air over his shoulder, while Jackie said, "He got one." I asked how he killed them and he said, "Old-timers would turn their heads inside out. New-timers like me figure they got a head, so club them."

On the way back down the beach we saw Floyd, one of Matt's brothers, plowing toward the horizon in a skiff. Matt said he was on his way to White Rock, an octopus ground against the shore of Chichagof Island.

I went to the store then for something to go with our lunch. Matthew Fred and Bessie, his wife, were in there, along with the Orthodox priest, who had come over for the weekend and was conducting a blessing of the place. The three of them and a couple of women I knew by sight, plus a woman who worked the cash register, formed a procession that went up and down the aisles, singing. The people shopping stepped aside for them. Bessie carried holy water in a peanut butter jar. The priest was dressed in a black robe with embroidered white cuffs and he was carrying an Orthodox cross. They came to a stop by the cake mixes and sang "God Grant You Many Years," which has a call-and-response part to it between high and low voices, but since Bessie was the only soprano, she sang the high part as a solo. The procession went upstairs and then into the basement, ducking their heads to fit through the low doorway and stepping aside for the conveyor belt that brought boxes up from storage. After they finished, the woman went back to the cash register and rung up my groceries while the others sang a hymn by the door, and then Matthew and Bessie and the priest climbed into Matthew's pickup and drove away.

That afternoon Jackie dressed up Nikolai and wrapped him in a blanket, and Matt put aside baiting and sharpening hooks, and the three of us and Nadja got in the truck and drove up the hill to Matthew Fred's house, where two other families had brought their babies to have the priest baptize them into the Orthodox Church. Before the ceremony the priest sat with the mothers at the dining-room table by the window looking out over the roofs of the town to the strait and told them that he would not be immersing the babies, but that the mothers should not be discouraged, because there was plenty of evidence in the Scriptures to back up the idea that baptism did not originally include immersion. Instead, people in former times would be brought to the river and stood waist-deep in it while water was poured over their heads.

"People try to say sometimes that you're not baptized if you weren't immersed," the priest said, "but these babies certainly will be."

The women nodded.

"Immersion is only for wicked people anyway," he said, "ones who need to be cleansed of their past. Sometimes a priest would hold that sort of person under until he fought to get up."

The women cradled their babies and looked their own selves like uncertain and obedient children.

"Now *that* would be a good way to fight for Christ,"

the priest went on. "We should all fight with that as an example. If you are ready to fight like that for Christ, you are ready to live the right life."

The priest was a large man with white hair and a trim beard and glasses. He was wearing a white robe with folds like curtains down the back. Matthew and Bessie had moved a table and a piano bench to clear a space on the rug in the center of the room. In it Matthew had placed a frame he had made to hold the galvanized tub he had earlier filled and left in the bathroom, intending that the water would settle to the temperature of the room. Matt and a man who was standing as a godfather carried it in. On a table beside the frame were a glass with a candle in it, a box holding the priest's paraphernalia, a watercolor brush, and a vial of oil. Around the edge of the tub were candles in holders. When the candles had been lit, the eleven older people, including Matt's mother, walked once around the tub. To keep devils from getting into the water, the priest stood beside it chanting prayers. Matthew gave everyone lighted candles. There were only two prayerbooks. The priest read from one and Matthew Fred controlled the other and made all the responses for the congregation. Occasionally, during a long recitation, he would lean over and say to the priest, *"Reading,* not chanting." Nikolai screamed when he was undressed. With the watercolor brush and the oil the priest painted crosses on the forehead and the cheeks and the shoulders and stomachs of each child, chanting as he did. In order to reach the tub he squatted and bent over from his waist. The strain on his back showed in a tremor as he held each child with one hand above the tub and with the other poured cupfuls of water over its head. Nikolai clutched the priest's neck and looked down at the water. Sunlight reflected off a tin roof next door. The room grew hotter with all the people, and there was the smell of a wet diaper. The priest said, "Thou art baptized, thou art illumined. Thou hast received the sacrament." And, "Thou art washed in the name of the Father, the Son, and the Holy Spirit." Bessie had me move a cross from the table after it was no longer needed, because as a woman she wasn't allowed to touch it. Then she told me to open a window, and a breeze came through. I watched a little girl fall off her bike, pick it up and wheel it hard and let it roll and crash into a ditch, then dust off her knees and run away. Bessie left the service and picked up the phone and gave someone instructions. The priest said, "Christ is risen," and everyone answered, "Indeed He is risen," and that was it.

Matthew Fred served everyone a glass of holy water from the tub and they drank it. We stepped outside just as a huge, long, fluttering rope of sandhill cranes was making its way over the town and out across the inlet.

THE next morning we had sourdough pancakes, then loaded bags of octopus from the freezer into a bait tub and stopped at the store for some dye Matt had ordered and went to the boat. Matt keeps his boat, the Sea Dance, at a dock off the lodge, both of which belong to his older brother, Albert. Garfield George and Mechanic Mike, a white man who fishes with Albert, were sitting on bait tubs on the dock, talking about places in the strait to put a set. It was about nine-thirty. Matt heated water for the dye, then filled a bait tub and dumped into it forty hooks and leaders, which were attached to the clips that join them to the groundline. This arrangement of hook, line, and clip the fishermen call a gangion, which is pronounced "gan-yen"; the groundline, with the gangions attached, they call a skate. Matt was hoping the leaders would turn red. Other fishermen had begun dyeing their leaders in the belief that it concealed them in the darkness at the bottom of the sea, but he had never dyed anything before and wasn't sure how it would go. Meanwhile he decided that the turn of the points on the hooks he was using from the year before was not severe enough, so he took about five hundred of them up the pier to Albert's workshop, and, one hook at a time, put them in the vise and bent the points back toward the shanks and hung each on the edge of the workbench. When he got back, around eleven, Matsu and Floyd were tying up at the end of the pier, having come from Hood Bay with herring. They had gone out at six and made three sets with a beach seine, and they had three tubs of herring in the bow of Matsu's whaler and the seine piled in the stern. On the way in, by Danger Point at the entrance to the inlet, they had passed killer whales. Floyd opened a beer and stood beside the boat, looking tired. Herring is the other popular halibut bait. It is fresher than octopus usually is, but not as tough, so a person using it has to bait his lines more than once. Matsu said people started using octopus when herring got scarce. "The bay used to bubble with herring," he said. "The bait-fishing industry depleted it. No one thought about octopus until herring turned hard to get."

Matt spent the afternoon dyeing his leaders. As it happened, he had nylon leaders and cotton dye, so they turned pink, which didn't bother him. He had had a line stolen the year before but couldn't do anything about it, since his were white and so were those of the boat he believed had taken them. Whenever he left, I had to take up a position on the deck to keep off the ravens and crows that would light in the rigging, and calculate the triangle involving them and me and the octopus in the bait tubs. Matsu salted his herring to preserve it, then baited hooks, using the whole herring, then cutting off the tails and tossing them in a pile to use when he ran out of fish. He gave some herring to Matt. While they worked, doll porpoises, which are about five feet long and black and white like killer whales, fed in the harbor. Chasing schools of herring, they would break the water in regular rhythms, looking with their fins rising and falling in half-circles like slowly turning saw blades.

After a while Matsu got tired of baiting. "Fishing is starting to turn to work," he said, "and it hasn't even started yet." To fish in his whaler, Matsu goes out the night before the opening to Chaik Bay, where a lot of small boats fish, and takes three cases of beer and parties with the other fishermen, then sleeps on the beach and wakes up early. If it rains, he sleeps under a tree.

MATT'S crew, Larry Knudson and Bob Schroeder, arrived late in the afternoon from Juneau, bringing Matt Jr., who was returning from a school trip to Washington, D.C. Larry is a carpenter in Juneau and lives with a Tlingit woman whom Jackie grew up with, and Bob works for Fish and Game in the Juneau office. They had crossed Chatham Strait on Bob's boat and were late, and Matt hadn't been able to raise them on the radio all afternoon. Larry and Bob are about in their forties and more or less opposite in every way. Bob is tall and Larry isn't. Bob has a beard and Larry doesn't. Bob talks slowly and soberly and likes to make sure everyone has heard every word he has said and has an academic's sense of precision in his speech, and Larry talks fast and easily and laughs as much as he talks, except when he is tired, and then he turns grave. Bob works in streaks and favors systems and the shortest way from one point to another, and Larry is relentless and dogged and inclined to pursue his curiosity as much as any system. Bob is a natural tutor and Larry a natural student. Both of them are funny and willing to work very hard, and the opposite aspects of their natures make them together form a strong crew. Larry is guileless and courteous and principled. It troubles him that by working for Matt he is taking a job from someone in Angoon, but Matt has already tried several people in town and not yet found anyone satisfactory, and his intention at fishing is to make money, not to be a benefactor to the town, except by spending there the money he makes. Even with an invitation, Larry will not hunt on islands where he knows that Tlingit resentment of white people hunting on their territory is high.

That night Jackie made lasagna for all of us, using sausage made from deer. Matt Jr. said that the question he got asked most often in Washington was whether he lived in an igloo. After dinner all of Matt and Jackie's nieces and nephews came over to celebrate Nik's birthday and the house was filled with kids. Larry and Bob slept on Bob's boat. When I went to bed, there were still people down at the dock, standing around by their boats with a beer can and a cigarette and talking to each other in the darkness.

W E left at three the next afternoon, heading up the inlet, then around Danger Point, into the strait, with Matt steering a-hundred-and-eighty degrees, and the boat drifting south with the tide. Matt had decided to spend the night in Kelp Bay, off Baranof Island.

Larry worked at the cleaning table in the middle of the deck, passing a file over the point of each hook, then baiting them and using his knife to cut off the ends of the longest tentacles. Facing the stern and rolling with the swells, he looked like a man taking punches. The swells came in pairs, with intervals of calm, then as if pausing to build themselves up, every fourth or fifth was about four feet, the spray washing across the deck and the back of Larry's yellow slicker. On the deck all you could hear besides the engine were the hiss of the wake and the scrape of the file. Matt Jr. slept in the cabin. Bob cleaned Matt's pistol on the galley table, then put it back on the shelf above the cabinets for the dishes. Matt said that some boat owners shoot the halibut as they come to the surface, especially the owners of smaller boats, because they are afraid of the trouble the big fish can cause. Sometimes out on the grounds, you hear the pop across the water in the darkness.

After we had been under way about forty-five minutes, the swells rose higher and turned to whitecaps, and it started to rain. A captain on the radio said a storm was coming in from the southeast, but Matt figured we would arrive in Kelp Bay before the worst of it. The only way I know not to get seasick is to stand on deck in the air, so I watched Larry work in the rain for a while and then the lower half of the mountains on Baranof started to come into view ahead through the fog, and the color of the shore began to change from blue-gray to green, and then I could pick out the single trunks of trees among the mass of the forest and then I could see the white head of an eagle in the top of a spruce.

Matt had planned to moor in Echo Cove, off North Point, but the weather was blowing into it, so he went across Kelp Bay, past South Point and into a cove sheltered by Pond Island, which was so protected that coming into it was like coming inside from a storm and closing the door. A boat called the Vulcan was already there. It had an aluminum hull that was shiny against the water. Three men stood on deck, baiting hooks, and they didn't even look at us. Matt moored about two hundred feet from them, up against a wilderness you couldn't see through the fog and rain.

Matt Jr. woke up with his hair sticking in several directions. Larry finished sharpening and baiting hooks and coiling them carefully in the bait tubs so they could be lifted out quickly and one at a time without tangling, then came in and slept for a while at the galley table beside Bob, who, wearing an Alaska Department of Fish and Game hat, was reading an article about bear attacks in *Sports Afield*. Matt sat at the galley table with charts spread before him, studying places in the strait for sets. Bob said it might be a good idea to put someone on deck to watch the birds, but Matt said there were no birds in that cove, and I was so surprised that he would know something so specific about a territory that I went outside to check, and he was right. When I got back in he was saying that last year he had seen a bear come down to the water on Pond Island and jump in and swim the channel to Baranof. We swung at anchor with the rain on the surface of the cove making small popping circles which expanded into rings the size of dinner plates and disappeared. Oystercatchers crossed the cove between us and the Vulcan, along with several small ducks of a kind called a butter-ball. Larry woke and picked up a small electric fan that was broken and was trying to figure a way to put the blade back together, when Matt told him to put it down. Matt enjoys being captain and having white guys to boss around. He named the man, known to Larry, who broke the fan, and he said, "Every white guy who comes on my boat breaks something."

That night we ate deer stew and cranberry muffins that Jackie had made. The stew was so hot it steamed up the windows. The galley table converts to a bed, which I shared with Larry. The bed was a piece of good fortune for me, since I had expected to sleep on the floor. When we got into it I could see the lights on the deck of the Vulcan and the men still baiting, but now also drinking beer. I heard the water lapping against the hull, and felt the rocking of the boat and heard the gas hissing in the pilot in the stove, and the clicking of the rain on the roof, and then I was asleep. Then someone on the radio was calling the Sea Dance and that woke everyone up, and it turned out to be the ship-to-shore operator on behalf of Bob's wife. He talked to her, for privacy, in some foreign language; later I asked if it was Spanish, and he said it was Nepali. I slept again for a while, and then Garfield George called and said he was out in the strait and wanted to know where Matt was anchored. Garfield had no radar and needed to know how to find the cove. Matt talked him in and he moored beside us. Then I tried to sleep some more, but Larry had a way of snoring that was more like a seizure than a snore, and I think I had just about fallen asleep when Matt came through the galley at five-thirty, saying, "You guys don't have to get up." Bob came in and said that he had dreamt about bear attacks. Matt made eggs and bacon and toast and coffee and there were more muffins, and Garfield came over and had breakfast with us. He had earned everyone's regard for crossing the strait at night with no radar and in some weather. Then Larry and Matt Jr. and Bob went to work baiting the rest of the hooks with herring, and somewhere around nine-thirty, the crew of the Vulcan, who had finished baiting the night before, appeared on deck, yawning and taking leaks over the gunwales. The mountains behind them looked as orderly and majestic as mountains in a landscape on the side of a van.

Matt planned to lay down first the sets for which there would be the most competition, and to save his others, which were secret and speculative. Mainly they were ones he had watched a captain from Juneau prosper with. The Juneau captain was especially aggressive, and the other fishermen tended to be afraid of him, so everyone gave him plenty of room. He had lately been in a car accident and Matt knew he wouldn't be out for the opening.

By the time we left the cove, around ten, other boats were showing up on the horizon. Through his binoculars, Matt could see that one of them was Albert and that he was sitting right in the middle of the set Matt hoped to make first. He picked another and began to trace its route slowly, to let the other boats know his intentions.

Sandhill cranes flew over us and across the strait, getting smaller and smaller, until they looked like perforations on a line saying Tear Here.

At ten-thirty, the Sailor, from Sitka, showed up, towing a raft. She circled us, while the captain, who was white, called out to ask if we had seen the St. Peter, the boat belonging to the captain who had been in the car accident; he was wondering whether it was safe to set in the area. Then he said that he planned to set outside the island, in the strait, which was also where Matt had thought of going. The horizon began to be highlighted by boats, like pins on a map. We spent the rest of the morning pointed at a ridge on Catherine Island, with the Sailor off our starboard bow, pointed in the same direction.

Ducks grazed the surface of the bay. The clouds lifted off the tops of the mountains. The wind stood at fifteen knots. Matt went in behind the Sailor, hoping to push him to declare his intentions. Garfield came on the radio and said, "Looks a little crowded out there." By now there were boats at even intervals all the way across the horizon. Garfield was holding a place against the island. The Sailor moved off toward Kelp Bay, leaving room for Matt in the strait. He stood on the flying bridge, watching the other boats through the glasses, hoping to preserve his first two sets.

The buoy for the first skate went over the stern precisely at twelve. Bob and Larry stood on either side of the skate as it payed out. They worked as fast as they could, clipping a gangion to the skate every twenty or thirty feet, then reaching into the bait tub for a new one. Each skate is about six hundred feet long, and where Matt was fishing they go down about eight or nine hundred feet. Off the stern an elephant seal surfaced and watched the line going out. A set takes about twenty-five minutes to complete. Matt put out four, then went to retrieve the first. In former times, when a Tlingit dropped a halibut hook over the side of his canoe, he would say, "Go right to the fireplace; hit the rich man's daughter."

Collecting the set, Matt worked the winch, bringing the skate to the surface. He bent over the stern from his waist, peering into the water for the stringy little gangion and the hook with or without bait, or with the fish. A fish coming up grows bigger and changes color and takes shape and comes into focus; it looks like a photograph assuming its form in a developing tray. When a hook came up with a fish, Matt Jr., standing beside his father, would remove the gangion and hang it from a cable running at shoulder-height above the gunwales. When he had a fish, Matt would grab the cable and yell "Fish," and steer the fish around to the side and club it between the eyes, and the fish would shudder and you could see it go blank, and then Larry or Bob would gaff it and wrestle it onto the deck. The largest of them were about five feet and weighed about a hundred and fifty pounds and did not always come over the side on the first try. Larry and Bob hoisted them on to the table in the middle of the deck, cleaned them, and threw them into the hold, which had ice in it. Sometimes when the fish were really coming in, the two of them got as many as eight fish behind, and sometimes there were lulls with no cleaning to do, when they would take out the hose and wash the slime and the blood off the table and the deck and their slickers. They worked with sharp knives, with the boat rocking in the swells, and with the flat, slippery bodies of the fish like carpets under their feet, but no one got cut. Once Matt had begun fishing, there were no more breaks. Anyone with a moment could wander into the galley and get something to eat or some coffee, but the fishing went on throughout the night and the next morning. In addition to halibut, black and gray cod took the bait, as well as rays, and yelloweye, whose eyes bulge out from the trip to the surface, and sometimes turbot, and a rockfish called an idiot, which was the fluorescent red color of a nail polish and was worth a dollar a pound. Sometimes sand fleas got to the fish first, and all that came up was a portion of the head attached to the hook and the spine with the bones sticking out, and the sand fleas dropping off it the color and shape of grains of rice. A squid came up holding on to one of the hooks, and Matt took it off and Larry picked it up. The squid flopped in his hands, and Larry said, "Hey, look at that, that's really a cute little thing, look, he's just *hey! hey! He bit me, Goddamnit, the thing just bit me, right through my glove, goddamnit look at that hole, the little bastard!"* and he swung his hand and the squid went cartwheeling into the air and over the side.

In the darkness all that one could see was the deck, and the deep-blue outline of the mountains on Baranof Island, and what portion of the water around was in the reach of the deck light, and the stars, and the points of light that were the other boats in the distance. Larry and Bob kept trading off jobs, to keep awake. For a while, early in the morning, the four of them worked under the huge, shimmering curtain of the northern lights.

THE sets alternated good and bad throughout the night. For a time it would look as if Matt had struck it rich, and then there would be a drought. One set came up with fewer than ten fish. Everyone worked steadily; to stop would be to acknowledge the cold and the quantities of water that had soaked through the cuffs of their gloves and down the necks of their slickers. The sun rose, but no one really noticed. Matt quit around eleven. He considered doing one more set, but thought he wouldn't be able to get it out of the water in time and didn't want to risk trouble with Fish and Game, so gave it up. On the way back to Angoon Larry finally sat down on a bucket of herring and leaned up against the cabin and went out.

We coasted round Danger Point and up the left side of the inlet where the deepest water was and into town on the most beautiful day I'd seen in Alaska. All the clouds were swept to the edges of the horizon, as if the sky were a great big dance floor, and you could see the details on the hills and a woman at a window in one of the houses watching us go by.

Matt and Bob and Larry delivered their fish to the buyer who had come over on the plane from Petersburg and set up shop at the boat harbor. She had a small sign that said, "Idiots $1 a pound." The price she quoted for halibut was disappointing, but there was a chance it might rise at the market. Matt had got fifty-one hundred pounds, the most, we learned later, of any boat in Angoon, but he had hoped for ten thousand. He was fishing for the year's payment on his boat, and didn't get it. The three of them spent the rest of the afternoon washing the boat down, then Larry left on the day's last plane, and Bob went out on his boat. When I went over to Matt's the next morning he told me he had gone to bed the night before at his regular time and got up at five-thirty, as usual, which impressed me, but I noticed that he walked around tired for about the next three days, and sometimes when you tried to get an answer from him, it was as if he had never heard the question. Whenever he sat down to mind Nikolai, his eyes started to focus into the distance.

For the next few days everyone in town was cleaning up his boat, and every time one man met another, the first thing he'd say was, "How'd you do halibut fishing?"


W A L K I N G one day through the burying ground at Killisnoo I came across a headstone about five feet tall and two feet wide. On the lower two-thirds was the clan image of a beaver, sitting on its haunches like a begging dog, its tail drawn up between its legs and its forepaws holding a log between its jaws, and above that, side by side on a narrow shelf carved from the stone, two portrait busts of a man. Except for the variations in the carver's hand, the images of the man were identical. He had his arms crossed, and he was posed as if leaning on a windowsill. His eyes were focused into the distance, which at the time he was buried would have been toward Killisnoo. Beneath the beaver was written Chief KI-TYCH-NA-TCH, SAGINAW JAKE,

Died 20, May 1908. I had never seen a tombstone anything like it before and was eager to know who Saginaw Jake was and what was the explanation for the two images, and when I got back to town I described it to an older woman I had met who I had been told was a regarded elder and asked her if she knew whether the man depicted on it was the man in the grave and whether she knew anything about him, and she said she had never seen the grave and knew nothing about a man by that name. Furthermore, she said, it would be an insult to a Tlingit to have his likeness appear on his grave. I asked Matt if he had ever heard of Saginaw Jake and he said, "There's a story behind all those graves, but no one remembers."

After I left Angoon I went to Juneau. Looking through a collection of photographs in the state historical library, I saw one of a small Indian man standing on a porch. He was wearing a military uniform and staring straight at the camera, and it was suddenly borne in on me that his was the face I had seen on the tombstone. He had a deformity which consisted of his left leg's being so much longer than his right that the buttons on the front of his coat traced a diagonal line down his chest. A sword hung from his belt. He stood in front of a door, using its frame as a backdrop. Above the door was a painted sign, which read:

> By the governor's commission
> And the company's permission,
> I'm made the Grand Tyee
> Of this entire illahee.
>
> Prominent in song and story,
> I've attained the top of glory;
> Saginaw Jake I'm known to fame,
> That is but my common name.

Eventually I learned that, along with two other Indians, Jake had been taken prisoner aboard the Saginaw as a result of a dispute at a coal mine near Angoon. The Navy operated coal mines to supply fuel for their steamers. The Saginaw went to San Francisco and took the Indians with them, and kept them there about four and a half months, then took them back and left them off at Angoon. During the time he was in San Francisco, Jake learned to speak English.

He was short, and squarely built, and bowlegged, and had a fondness for military and ceremonial dress. In time he was made chief of police at Killisnoo and given a uniform and a salary and a place to live. Whenever a tourist ship arrived, he put on a costume and went down to the pier and walked back and forth. He would wear a general's uniform that was decorated on the chest with stars, or his police uniform, or a Russian monk's cassock and cowl, or an admiral's uniform. Sometimes he would wear one outfit for a few minutes and then race up to his house and change and come back in another.

In addition to his place in Killisnoo, Jake also had a house in Angoon. After his first wife died, he married a second, who was much younger. From where he lived in Killisnoo he could see the cross marking the ashes of his first wife.

He married the second wife in 1885, when he was approximately fifty and she was about fifteen. Jake gave the bride's father ten new camphor-scented scarlet blankets. He was married in the Orthodox church in Killisnoo, and the governor of Alaska came to his wedding. Among the gifts was a book of colored engravings illustrating the life of Christ.

During the time when he was modeling his uniforms on the dock he would pose for photographs, provided he was the only one in them. His second wife used to like to be in them also, but he would not permit her to be. When she got angry enough about this she would return to her father's house, and Jake would have to pay her father blankets to get her to return.

Jake had been engaged to appear at the Alaska Yukon Pacific Exposition held at Seattle in 1909 to display his uniforms, hats, and decorations, but he died too soon. The obituary in the Juneau paper said that a few years before his death he had ordered a fancy extra-large coffin, in which he built compartments to store his regalia. He had a terror of being buried alive, and left instructions to his survivors that if they thought he was dead, they were to put a cannon close to his coffin and fire it at intervals for a week. If he didn't wake up, they could bury him.


BETWEEN 1867 and 1884, Alaska had no government. It was described by someone who lived in Sitka at the time as being "almost as free from the operation of civil law as the interior of Africa." The United States kept a warship in the harbor at Sitka, and word was sent to its commander when a problem on shore required his intervention. In 1879 a miner shot a man in broad daylight on a street in Sitka in front of a dozen witnesses. Although the miner meant to kill him, the man survived. The commander of the warship had the miner arrested and sent for trial to Portland, Oregon, where the judge released him, saying that in Alaska all that applied were statutes covering piracy and whatever other acts the government in Washington had specified, and attempted murder was not one of them.

The warship stationed in Sitka in the late eighteen-seventies and early eighteen-eighties was the Jamestown and its commander was L. A. Beardslee. The Jamestown was too large to maneuver among the channels of the archipelago. Whenever it became necessary to pursue anyone, her crew would board steam launches, which were not able to carry many men or to travel any distance. The launches could use only fresh water, which meant that they had to stop every four hours at a waterfall or a creek and while they were filling up they were liable to attack from the forest. Beardslee decided that the white people were better off gaining control of the Tlingit by means of good will and with their consent, since the Tlingit, if they acted together, could overwhelm Sitka, and also any prospectors in the wilderness.

Because Beardslee thought it a bad and provocative idea to have white men arresting Indians, he set up a native police to handle calls in the Indian village. His observations of the Tlingit convinced him that they valued strict justice and that an Indian given a chance to defend himself would accept any punishment, however severe.

He wrote that what was needed for southeast Alaska was a government strong enough to restrain disorderly drunks, white or Indian, and protect the rest of the community from harm. As it happened, the Indians needed protection much more often than the whites. In one month in 1879 the Tlingit in Sitka registered a thousand complaints against the whites, but there was no authority there to do anything about them.

Beardslee felt that until he was given a better example by the federal government of how to treat the Tlingit, he must rely on their laws. If a man was murdered and his relations settled it with his killer by means of a payment, then Beardslee felt he must consider the case dispatched.

He began his final report, which was for the year 1880,

by saying, "I think that the period has arrived when it becomes my duty to report that in my judgment the permanent retention of a vessel of war at this place is no longer a necessity. Such detention could only be required through a duty of protecting helpless whites from the assaults of dangerous Indians, neither of which conditions now exist."

He wrote that the whites were capable of bearing arms and that the number of Indians returning from the wilderness at the end of the hunting season was offset by the miners and prospectors returning at the same time. Nearly every white man in town employed an Indian for one reason or another, and Beardlsee felt that this would cause the Indian in the case of trouble to be loyal, either through friendship or dependency. Also many of the white men had Indian mistresses, who Beardslee believed would argue against harm to the whites. As evidence that whites and Indians could live together, he mentions the Hootsnoowoos. Lack of place pride, he says, was what really hindered the whites: " 'Each man for himself' is their motto; and their town becomes filthy; the wooden sidewalks rotten, limb-breaking traps; their bridges ruins; and their schools and church a failure, if unsupported by others; . . . Dance-houses, gambling hells, rum-selling saloons, and houses of prostitution exist on the main street, and no man puts forth an effort against them."

The white people of Alaska had no wish to pay taxes to support a government, or to have their alcohol trade or that of selling the ingredients for hoochinoo to the Indians interfered with, or to have drunks arrested. The event that as much as any other factor finally brought government to Alaska was the destruction of Angoon by the Navy in 1882.

. . .

THE customs officer at Sitka, a man named William Morris, liked to point his gun through a window on the second floor of his house and shoot dogs on the steps of the houses in the Indian village. An issue of the New York *Times* for October 12, 1882, refers to his hobby as the "ruthless slaughter of Indian dogs." On one occasion the Indians surrounded his house and threatened to destroy it. The naval officer who followed Beardslee in command of the Jamestown described Morris as arbitrary and aggressive in his behavior toward the Indians and said that he exercised authority in a way that was unwarranted and overbearing. He also said that if Morris were allowed to remain in his position the result would likely be "a serious outbreak among the Indians." The other naval officers accused Morris of being a bootlegger.

Beardslee's replacement was Henry Glass, the man who took pleasure in humiliating Tlingit shamans, and he in turn was replaced by E. C. Merriman, in command of the Adams. He made his first visit to Killisnoo in the September of 1882, in order to raid Indian stills and seize any hoochinoo he could find. Not long before he arrived, an Indian cutting down a tree for the Northwest Trading Company had run back for his jacket as the tree was falling and the tree had fallen on him. As was Tlingit practice, his relatives demanded a payment from the company, whom they held responsible. The payment they asked for was one hundred blankets. The company refused to pay anything. When Merriman arrived, the superintendent complained about the Indians' demand. Merriman told the Indians that no demands of the kind should be made anymore on white people and that the company would not pay in this instance and that if the relatives pushed it any further he would see they were punished severely. "They submitted with bad grace," is how Morris described it.

On the night of October twenty-second, a party of Indians and two white men, E. H. Boyne and S. S. Stulzman, fishing for the Northwest Trading Company, were chasing a whale through the inlet when the explosive in their whale gun went off and killed Tith Klane, a Tlingit shaman who was standing behind the gun. It is a Tlingit custom that any objects involved in the death of a man must be retired for three days, a period of mourning. The other Indians on the whaleboat took the boat into shore, along with the fishing nets and the whale gun, and kept them, and kept the two white men, saying that they would not give them up until they were paid two hundred blankets, one hundred for the death of the logger and one hundred for the death of the shaman. At some point another boat belonging to the company was seized, along with a steam launch. The company superintendent collected his family on board the tugboat Favorite and took off for Sitka. When he arrived, on the afternoon of the twenty-third, he told Merriman that the Indians were holding the boats and two prisoners and that they were demanding two hundred blankets and threatened to burn the company's store and other buildings, destroy the boats, and kill the white men if they didn't get them. Merriman loaded a howitzer and a Gatling gun, the first in Alaska, onto the Favorite, which left for Killisnoo at three o'clock on the morning of the twenty-fourth. Because the Adams was too drafty for the inlet M. A. Healy, the commander of the Corwin, a revenue steamer coaling in Sitka, offered the use of his boat, and Merriman accepted. At seven that same morning Merriman, Morris, and about a hundred marines steamed off in the Corwin for Killisnoo. The weather was so rough they spent the night in a harbor near the entrance to Peril Strait. They arrived in Killisnoo on the morning of the twenty-fifth. For some reason they stayed there a day and the next morning, that is, the twenty-sixth, Merriman wrote out orders for Lieutenant Bartlett, in command of the Favorite.

> Sir: Proceed up the lagoon behind the Indian village of Angoon, and upon your arrival with the Favorite ... rescue the employes of the Northwest Trading Company, now held by the Indians, their steam launch and such property as the Indians have belonging to this company. They will at first probably attempt to take charge of the Favorite, thinking only the employes are on board. Treat the Indians kindly if they show a peaceful disposition. With the Corwin I shall proceed off the town. Should the Indians show fight attack them vigorously, blow three long blasts of the whistle of both steamers, and fire *two* guns; one gun I shall look at simply as a show of force from you. Should the Indians be on *our* side of the town a *second* gun from the Corwin will denote that we will attack. In the first case we will come to your support, in the second you will come to ours. Get possession of every canoe you can, and get all the Indians to come to the white settlement possible. The cause of the outbreak is the accidental killing of an Indian by the premature explosion of a whaling bomb. They demand two hundred blankets as damages. On the contrary, I propose to fine them four hundred, or double what their claim may be. In case of refusal I have determined to burn their village and destroy their canoes and fishing tackle. Remember in the *first place* to free their white prisoners, and secondly the property. Should the Indians forcibly resist after knowing your intentions, do not hesitate; open fire at once, and I will immediately come to your support in the Corwin. Use

all diplomacy possible first, however. I rely on your discretion, and wish you a most successful trip.

The white men and the boats, it turned out, were not being held at Angoon, but at a summer fishing village on Kootznahoo Inlet, which was where Merriman and Healy had gone in the Corwin. "Immediately we anchored, the white men were released." Healy wrote. The Indians also gave up the boats and the fishing gear. Merriman took two of the clan chiefs on board. "I held a powwow with the Indians," he wrote. The Indians asked for their two hundred blankets, and Merriman told them they were not going to get them. "I had explained to them on my previous visit the fallacy of any claim when the death was purely accidental. I ascertained that they had attempted to destroy the boats, and that they were only waiting for another white man to put two to death. One of the men captured had but one eye, and they wanted a whole one, or one with two eyes." Merriman then told them that they must pay him four hundred blankets, and that they would have twenty-four hours to produce them, and that if they failed to he would destroy their canoes and their village.

Exactly how much the Indians understood is not clear, since Merriman did not bring a translator, and the Indians understood little English. Merriman said that the Indians returned to Angoon and sent word back that they had no intention of paying the fine, and would fire at any marines who attacked. He said that the Tlingit drew their canoes up into the woods and took their winter food and blankets and their women and children with them and deserted the town. That is perhaps not the truth. Merriman's account of the bombing appears in a letter to the Secretary of the Treasury, delivered to Congress on January 8, 1883, and dated, from Sitka, on October 28, 1882. Someone familiar with several accounts of the event is given more than one reason to believe that Merriman altered his story of the bombardment. Merriman said that he did not begin shelling until he had found out, without the Indians' knowing that he had, that all the women and children were out of the town. It was said by some people at the time, however, that Merriman had sent marines into the woods behind the town to keep the Tlingit from escaping into the forest. Merriman claims to have given the Tlingit twenty-four hours to respond, but a woman who spoke to him on his return to Sitka said that he told her he had shelled the Indians two hours after issuing his demand—that is, at the moment he found out they intended not to pay. If she is right, the bombardment took place on the twenty-sixth. If he is right, it took place the twenty-seventh. What is also known is that Lieutenant Bartlett rounded up from the beach in front of Angoon about forty of the Tlingits' canoes. These were tied together and towed out into the water and then the marines fired on them with the Gatling gun. The marines missed, apparently again and again, so they were sent back with augers, and the canoes were towed into Chatham Strait and the marines bored holes in them and sank them in deep water.

Meanwhile Merriman burned the Indians' summer camp and its store of food to the ground. Then he weighed anchor and steamed round to Angoon and opened fire. Under cover of the guns, he landed marines on the beach who poured kerosene over what was left of the houses that had been struck by shells and set them on fire and also set other houses on fire. They also burned the Indians' store of food and oil for the winter. Merriman claimed that of the twenty-nine houses in Angoon, he destroyed twenty, saving nine that belonged to Indians sympathetic to the white man. The Indians claim he destroyed the whole town. What is also known is that the marines who set fire to the houses first robbed them of blankets and clan ornaments and anything else that caught their eyes, and by pointing guns at the owners of the houses kept back the Tlingit who tried to save their possessions. Knowing that there were no means of fighting any fires, one wonders if it was possible for any houses in a village of houses built so closely together to survive a conflagration.

"After burning the town," Merriman wrote, "I directed the Indians to come to the trading post, where I would talk to them. A crowd came at about 8 P.M., with the chief Kanalkos and Loginon Jake." Who Merriman means is Saginaw Jake. "I told them in substance what I had said before, that while the government felt friendly to them and wanted them to till the soil and fish and hunt, and would protect them in pursuing their peaceful avocations, it would put down with a rigorous hand any attempt to seize and injure white men or their property, or to distill rum. They replied that they would never attempt anything of the kind again; that the old men and the chiefs had tried to restrain the young men, but were unable to do so; that as a lesson to the young men and squaws they were glad I had burned the village. To those who had rendered service to the whites by protecting them I gave small presents. To one old medicine-man and herculean squaw, who had quietly brought their guns to the white men's cabins and declared their intention of defending them and the property of the trading company, I gave letters, with large seals attached, recounting their services. I am told they think more of these than anything else, as it gives them much importance in the tribes."

·   ·   ·

M O R R I S , the dog-shooter, the bootlegger, also wrote a letter to the Secretary of the Treasury, which was dated, from Sitka, November 9, 1882, and passed on to Congress on December 21, 1882. His letter begins:

"Sir: On the 28th of last month I had the honor to transmit to the department the following telegram:

'26th inst. Hoochenoo Indians becoming troublesome, capturing property from whites, Commander Merriman repaired thither in Corwin. Became necessary to shell and destroy village, canoes, and make prisoners. Severe lesson taught. Particulars by mail.'

After giving his version of the bombardment, Morris wrote, "As long as the native tribes throughout the archipelago do not feel the force of the government and are not punished for flagrant outrages, so much the more dangerous do they become, and are to be feared by isolated prospecting parties of miners. Once let it be understood by the Siwashes"—white slang for Indians—"that the life of a white man is sacred, and that they will be severely handled if they harm him, there will be no danger or difficulty in small parties traversing the country in search of mineral and other wealth."

One result of the bombardment was predictable. This is an excerpt from a letter written by a miner from Juneau a few years after the event. He misspells "Merriman."

"Many prospectors and hunters who went to the neighborhood of Admiralty Island after that were never heard of again, and it is believed that they suffered death at the hands of the Indians of the Hootchinoo tribe as vengeance for the inhumanity of Captain Berryman and his marines and sailors."

The most remarkable omission from the accounts of Healy, Morris, and Merriman is that after the bombardment six children were dead. The totem poles in the center of Angoon were raised to their memory during the commemoration of the bombing held in 1982.

A MAN named I. S. Oakford, who questioned one of the men held hostage, was told that the Indians never abused him or even threatened to. They told him only that he would not be allowed to return to Killisnoo or to take the steam launch back until the two hundred blankets had been delivered. Oakford wrote in a letter, "The wanton destruction of the Indian houses and canoes is condemned by everyone here, except by that class of white men whose creed is summed up in the words 'That the Indians have no rights which a white man is bound to respect.' "

MERRIMAN had more courage facing an outgunned group of Indian families than he did when dealing with white men. Not long before, he had been called to Juneau to intervene in a difficulty at a mine. He anchored his ship in the harbor off the mine and told the miners that if they did not quit work within twenty-four hours, he would open fire on them. The miners said that if he did not pull out of there, they would float a box of powder under his stern and blow up his ship. Merriman waited for darkness to fall and quietly slipped away.

WORD of the bombardment reached Washington by the beginning of December. On December 4, the House of Representatives passed a resolution requesting information from the Secretary of the Treasury, first to know whether it was true that a revenue cutter had shelled two Alaskan villages (Angoon and the summer camp), and if so, for what reason, and under whose orders. That is how the letters from Healy, Merriman, and Morris came to be published. By the spring of 1884 the letters were a part of the debate on the need for law in Alaska. On May 13, on the floor of the House, Representative James Budd, from California, referred first to the letter written by Healy, then the others. "This report is furnished by one of the men who shelled the village," he said, "and consequently may be expected to be colored in their favor. But notwithstanding this, these reports show this to have been the greatest outrage ever committed in the United States upon any Indian tribe."

DURING the October of 1982, on the twenty-fourth, the twenty-fifth, and the twenty-sixth, Angoon held a series of ceremonies to commemorate the hundredth anniversary of the bombing. The governor signed a proclamation declaring October 26 Tlingit Remembrance Day. In 1973 the Tlingit and Haida Central Council, on behalf of the people of Angoon, had brought a suit against the government before the Indian Claims Commission. The law under which they were able to press their case allowed damages only for clan and tribal property and only at the 1882 value. They were prevented from asking for any damages for loss of life, or property belonging to individuals, or for the emotional consequences or suffering. Nine days before the trial was to open, the government offered to settle the claim for ninety thousand dollars. The Tlingit thought about it a while. What they really wanted was to amend the law so that it would cover what it excluded, but they decided that this was not a realistic possibility and accepted the offer.

A delegation from Angoon met in Washington with

the Assistant Secretary of the Navy, in hopes of receiving an apology, but they did not get one. What they got was a letter from the Assistant Secretary saying, among other things, "The destruction of Angoon should never have happened and it was an unfortunate event in our history."

People in Angoon talk of putting up a ridicule pole to the Navy, tall enough that it could be seen from Chatham Strait. What they want, and realize they will probably never get, is a ship in the Navy named for their village.

MATTHEW FRED speaking: "They said it was an accident, that the gun they shoot the whale with hit him, but how can you shoot a man on a boat with a gun unless you point it at him?

"It's no accident anyway when you saturate buildings with kerosene. It's no accident when you destroy all our boats. It's no accident when you turn guns on women and children. It's no accident when you shell a village. It's not an accident when you burn houses with torches. It's not an accident when you take winter provisions—smoked salmon and deer meat and seal meat—and throw them into the water with the tide. It's not an accident when you carry the loot down to the boat and throw it on your ship. It's not an accident when you kill children.

"That medicine man was of nobility, so everything has to be quiet for three days; this is the equivalent of a minute of silence, but ours is three days. The manager went to Sitka and brought back the Navy, and all our menfolks were inside the bay getting herring, that's when the Navy started the shelling. They had just received a new weapon, and that was the Gatling gun, and they were itching to use it. They came ashore and looted our buildings before they set them on fire, a lot of our ancient artifacts were snook out. The Navy went up the inlet where our food caches were, on dry ground, and they threw them into the water. My uncle was on the hill where the Orthodox church is and he saw our provisions going out on the tide. He saw the Navy pouring kerosene on the buildings and throwing torches on them. He saw them busting up the war canoes, and going up the bay and burning the camp and busting up our rifles. When the men from the village came back, there were smoking buildings. The boats they had for fishing were the only things we had to use to get food. So it actually took us ten years before we got back on our feet, five years just to heal up the wounds and five more years to recover and rebuild our village. It was never recorded how many people died from hunger and exposure. We just had to throw buildings together from the lumber we could find on the beach.

"Ninety thousand is not a proper settlement for houses burned and property damaged, and looting of our village. They stole from us. They still haven't paid us for our belongings. Blankets were our currency. They knew the men were out gathering up stores for the winter and had no time for counterattacks.

"We were never conquered or defeated by the U.S. or the Russians. Each Tlingit community is a sovereign nation and that's the way it was, and that's what we believe. If the Navy wants to call that a victory, what they shelled was the women and children and old men, if they want to be proud of it, that's their business."


IN 1950 Frederica De Laguna, an anthropologist, used a tape recorder and an interpreter to take down a version of the bombardment from a man who had been a child at the time. What follows is perhaps half of what he said.

"I would like you to hear me, respectable people. . . . I am already an old man. I was a young man when our village was spoiled. White people spoiled it. They left us homeless on the beach. . . . My name is Languc-'u, 'Homeless Raven.' That is the man who is telling you the story now. . . .

"At the time people were living on the other side [on Kootznahoo Inlet]. They were putting up herring. When the boat came to that side, they smashed up all the Indian canoes—broke them up. No more. When the Coast Guard came back they set the town afire. They were anchored right outside this village. No more. My mother said to me, 'Do you understand what is happening?' And I said, 'Yes, I understand.'

"Six children—no more. They were suffocated by the smoke, the ones that stayed in the village. The smoke killed them. All the food was destroyed: blankets, clothing, many houses—no more. Nothing was saved. Countless things in the houses were all burned up.

"I did not see why this happened, what it was that made them treat us like that. We were defenseless, but they came to punish us for nothing. They took everything out of the houses aboard the Coast Guard boat. They said it was punishment. See how great our trouble was. I am going to be silent for a while."

De Laguna notes that the man who was speaking was overcome by emotion and paused until able to go on.

"Now hear what I am telling," he said next. "When the fall was coming, when the winter was beginning, the people of Angoon nearly starved to death, all of them. How much we suffered! . . .

"I am going to add something of my own—a moral. If a man did that, if a Tlingit did that to someone, what would you say, Government? If someone did this to you?

This is what I ask you: what are you going to say if some-one did this to *you?*

"That is all. That is the end of the story of how trouble came to us and we never received help from the government. That is the end."

The man stopped here and spoke in Tlingit to the people he was with and then added:

"You have been listening to my words. You are white people and we are Tlingit. You have taken a black cloth and covered our eyes with it, hiding our land. The Tlingit did not give you permission to take all of Alaska. You bought it from the Russians, but not all of it, only the places that the Russians owned. That was what you bought. . . .

"This is our land. They always tell us, any land we claim, anything we take from it—we have to pay you taxes. Even if we kill a deer, it is not good for us. The bears are killing all the deer; the wolves are killing them off. See how everything is being killed. You white people, see how much you have destroyed!

"The things in the water, you have destroyed. . . . But just the same, whenever there is going to be a war, you take our children by the hand without a word. You take them for death. I do not know why. . . .

"When you are going to make laws, you never consult us Tlingit. . . . You make it in secret, and then just tell us that the law is made. . . .

"We, who are old people, always feel very sad. My-self, I'm not strong enough to kill anything anymore. I'm all through. I am speaking for the last time. This is the end of my speech, of my words."

.   .   .

THERE is a Tlingit song called Big-Song, sung at certain clan feasts after a rich man had died. As they sang, the mourners all turned round to face the sun.

I am now saying just as the man I live after, Dātxagu'tte, used to say.
This song is from sand-hill town.
We are the people who feel higher than all others in the world.

# Acknowledgments

In addition to the people whose names appear in the text, I am grateful to these others for their help or consideration:

At *The New Yorker:* Robert Gottlieb, Charles McGrath, Patrick Crow, James Albrecht, Adam Gopnik, Deborah Garrison, Martha Kaplan, Sheila McGrath, John McPhee, Natasha Turi, William Shawn, Nancy Boensch, and Bruce Diones.

At Knopf: Ann Close, Ann Kraybill, Paul Bogaards, Nicholas Latimer, and William Loverd.

Elsewhere: Andrew Wylie, Sarah Chalfant, Candy Jernigan, Julie Carlson, Robert De Armond, Bob Price, William Maxwell, and Saul Steinberg.

Whatever information about the Tlingits, Alaska, or any other subject covered in "The Uncommitted Crime" that did not come from interviews, was drawn from the following sources:

## Acknowledgments

ANDERSON, SUSAN, *The Great Angoon Cookbook.* Jumbo Jack's Cookbook Company, Audubon, Iowa, 1990.

BABBIT, ANGELICA, *Board of Education Report for Killisnoo, Alaska.* Alaska State Historical Archives, Juneau, 1900s.

BEARDSLEE, L. A., reports of . . . , relative to affairs in Alaska, and the operation of the U.S.S. *Jamestown,* 47th Cong., 1st Sess., Sen. Ex. Doc., No. 71, in vol. 4, 1882.

BERGER, THOMAS, *Village Journey.* Hill and Wang, New York, 1985.

COBB, JOHN, *Pacific Salmon Fisheries.* U.S. Government Printing Office, Washington, D.C., 1930.

*Congressional Record,* May 13, 1884, remarks of Senator Budd, p. 4123.

DE ARMOND, ROBERT N., "Saginaw Jake," *Alaska History,* Spring 1990.

DAVIDSON, FREDERICK, AND SHOSTROM, EUGENE, *Physical and Chemical Changes in the Pink Salmon During the Spawning Migration.* United States Government Printing Office, Washington, D.C., 1936.

EMMONS, G. T., "The Tlingit Indians," unpublished manuscript. Archives, American Museum of Natural History, New York, n.d.

FITZHUGH, WILLIAM, AND CROWELL, ARON, *Crossroads of Continents.* Smithsonian Institution Press, Washington, D.C.

*GARFIELD, VIOLA, "Historical Aspects of Tlingit Clans in Angoon, Alaska," *Amer. Anthrop.,* 1947, vol. 49, pp. 438–52.

GARFIELD, VIOLA, AND FORREST, LINN, *The Wolf and the Raven.* University of Washington Press, Seattle, 1948.

GEORGE, GABRIEL, AND BOSWORTH, ROBERT, *Use of Fish and Wildlife by Residents of Angoon, Admiralty Island, Alaska.* Alaska Department of Fish and Game, Technical Paper no. 159, 1988.

GEORGE, GABRIEL, AND KOOKESH, MATTHEW, *Salt Lake Coho Subsistence Permit Fishery.* Alaska Department of Fish and Game, Technical Paper no. 70, 1982.

GLASS, HENRY, NAVAL ADMINISTRATION IN ALASKA. *Proceedings of the United States Naval Institute,* 1890, vol. XVI, no. 1, no. 52: 1–19.

GMELCH, GEORGE AND SHARON, *Resource Use in a Small Alaskan City.* Alaska Department of Fish and Game, Technical Paper no. 90, 1985.

GOLDSCHMIDT, WALTER R., AND HAAS, THEODORE H., *Possessory Rights of the Natives of Southeastern Alaska.* A Report to the Commissioner of Indian Affairs. (Mimeographed). Washington, D.C., 1946.

GOODHEART, R., *Board of Education Report for Killisnoo, Alaska.* Alaska State Historical Archives, Juneau, 1913.

HEALY, M. A., "Alleged Shelling of Alaskan Villages," extract of a letter . . . , Nov. 20, 1882, 47th Cong. 2nd Sess., House Ex. Doc., no. 9, in vol. 14.

HOLM, BILL, *The Box of Daylight.* University of Washington Press, Seattle, 1983.

JACKSON, SHELDON, Statements Before a Subcommittee of the Committee on Territories, 1880.

——, *Alaska.* Dodd, Mead & Co., New York, 1880.

——, *Report on Education in Alaska for Department of the Interior,* Alaska State Historical Archives, Juneau, 1881.

ᵇ JONAITIS, ALDONA, *Art of the Northern Tlingit.* University of Washington Press, Seattle, 1986.

ᶻ JONES, LIVINGSTON, *A Study of the Thlingets of Alaska.* New York: Fleming H. Revell Co., 1914.

KAMENSKII, FR. ANATOLII, *Tlingit Indians of Alaska.* Translated, with an introduction and supplementary material by Sergei Kan, University of Alaska Press, 1985 [originally published in Russian in 1906].

KAN, SERGEI, "Wrap Your Father's Brothers in Kind Words," unpublished Ph.D. dissertation in anthropology, University of Chicago, 1982.

᾽ KNAPP, FRANCES, AND CHILDE, RHETA, *The Thlinkets of Southeastern Alaska.* Stone and Kimball, Chicago, 1896.

᾽ KRAUSE, AUREL, *The Tlingit Indians.* Translated by Erna Gunther, University of Washington Press, Seattle, 1970 [originally published in German in 1885].

LAGUNA, FREDERICA DE, "Some Dynamic Forces in Tlingit

Society," *Southwestern Journal of Anthropology,* vol. 8, 1952, pp. 1–12.

————, *The Story of a Tlingit Community.* Native American Book Publishers, Brighton, Michigan, 1960.

————, *Under Mt. St. Elias,* vols. 1–3. Smithsonian Institution Press, Washington, D.C., 1972.

LANGDON, STEPHEN, "Technology, Ecology, and Economy: Fishing Systems in Southeast Alaska," unpublished Ph.D. dissertation, Stanford University, 1977.

MERRIMAN, E. C., *Affairs in Alaska,* Report of . . . , October 28, 1882. 47th Cong., 2nd Sess., House Exec. Doc., no. 9, pt. 3, in vol. 14, 1883.

————, Letter to Sheldon Jackson, Sheldon Jackson Correspondence File, Presbyterian Historical Society, Philadelphia, 1883.

MORRIS, WILLIAM GOUVERNEUR, *Report upon the Customs District, Public Service, and Resources of Alaska Territory.* 45th Cong., 3rd Sess., Sen. Exec. Doc., No. 59, 1879.

————,"Shelling of an Indian Village in Alaska," letter by . . . , Nov. 9, 1882. 47th Cong., 2nd Sess., House Exec. Doc., No. 9, pt. 2, in Vol. 14, 1882.

MUIR, JOHN, TRAVELS IN ALASKA. Cambridge, Mass., 1915.

OBERG, KALVERVO, "The Social Economy of the Tlingit Indians," unpublished Ph.D. dissertation, University of Chicago, 1937.

OLSON, RONALD, *Social Structure and Social Life of the Tlingit Indians in Alaska.* University of California Anthropological Records 26, 1967.

RATHBURN, ROBERT, "Processes of Russian-Tlingit Acculturation in Southeastern Alaska," unpublished Ph.D. dissertation, University of Wisconsin, 1976.

REPLOGLE, CHARLES, *Among the Indians of Alaska.* Headley Brothers, London, 1904.

ROTHENBURG, JEROME (editor), *Shaking the Pumpkin.* Alfred van der Marck Editions, New York, 1986.

SALISBURY, O. M., *Quoth the Raven.* Superior Publishing Co., Seattle, 1962.

SCIDMORE, E. RUHAMAII, *Alaska: Its Southern Coast and the Sitkan Archipelago.* D. Lothrop and Co., Boston, 1885.

STEWART, HILARY, *Looking at Indian Art of the Northwest Coast.* University of Washington Press, Seattle, 1979.

SWANTON, JOHN R., "Social Conditions, Beliefs, and Linguistic Relationships of the Tlingit Indians," in 26th Annual Report of the Bureau of American Ethnology, 1908. Washington, D.C.: U.S. Government Printing Office. pp. 391–486.

——, "Tlingit Myths and Texts," Bureau of American Ethnology Bulletin 39, 1909, Washington, D.C.: U.S. Government Printing Office.

THURLEY, ISABELLE, *Board of Education Report for Killisnoo, Alaska.* Alaska State Historical Archives, Juneau, 1909.

UNITED STATES GOVERNMENT, Military Reconnaissance in Alaska, 48th Cong., 2nd Sess., Sen. Exec. Doc., no. 2, 1884.

WOOD, C. E. S., "Among the Thlinkets in Alaska," *The Century Magazine,* vol. XXIV, July, 1882.

A NOTE ON THE TYPE

The text of this book was set in a digitized version of Bembo,
the well-known monotype face. The original cutting of
Bembo was made by Francesco Griffo of Bologna only a few
years after Columbus discovered America. It was named
after Pietro Bembo, the celebrated Renaissance writer and
humanist scholar who was made a cardinal and served as
secretary to Pope Leo X. Sturdy, well-balanced, and finely
proportioned, Bembo is a face of rare beauty. It is, at the
same time, extremely legible in all of its sizes.

Composed by Creative Graphics, Inc.
Allentown, Pennsylvania

Printed and bound by The Haddon Craftsmen, Inc.,
Scranton, Pennsylvania

Typography and binding design by
Dorothy S. Baker